# Culinary English Skill Builder

## 조리영어 스킬 빌더

Jonathan Huynh
Ra Young-Sun

# Preface

As the world has become increasingly interconnected, more opportunities have risen for sharing knowledge, sourcing learning through materials printed in other languages and for working with international others. Accordingly, a number of pragmatic reasons for culinary arts professionals to take interest in the study of English as a foreign language can be observed: some will have interest in sourcing their work from other cuisines' recipes that are printed in English, and some will want to share their favorite recipes with English speaking colleagues and friends, or promote their cuisines with broader groups of international others. Some will pursue opportunities for study or work in the contexts for which they have specialized their culinary studies, and all are likely to find themselves in situations in which they must communicate about their work with guests in professional settings.

There does however exist some challenges when it comes to gaining skills in very specific areas of the English language. If an individual wants to learn English language communication, grammar or testing skills, a plethora of materials exist for study. Similarly, there exist texts for culinary arts professionals of advanced English language skills and those that work and live in contexts where English is spoken as the primary language. Although many such materials provide excellent and necessary content knowledge, many neglect the more foundational language skills required for accessing or producing such language at beginner and intermediate levels. It is with those thoughts and the practical English language needs of culinary arts professionals in English foreign language learning contexts in mind that the materials and exercises in this book were developed.

# Outline and Design Notes

This book is designed for use by culinary arts students and professionals. It provides exercises that encourage reflection on professional knowledge and development of corresponding English language skills. Some of this book's target language is prescriptive; however, owing to the broad nature of the culinary art, many of this book's exercises call on learners to explore and develop the English language skills most individually relevant.

Because most Culinary Arts students and professionals will work in the back of house of local kitchens and hotel restaurants, the first section focuses on promoting the language skills required to access English language recipes from which they can source their work. Recipes are concise instructions: each word of a recipe imparts important meaning to cooking processes. The first section's exercises thus focus on promoting lexical knowledge and takes a scaffolding approach to language learning—starting simple and layering the elements needed to proceed to later units' more detailed exercises. These units encourage creativity, while emphasizing the importance of detail, such that is necessary for precision and consistency in restaurant service.

It is important for culinary arts professionals to be able to discuss and describe their and other chefs' work, and explore responses to new food trends, introduce local cuisines to foreign audiences, and carry out general interactions with guests in a restaurant's front of house. The second section of this book thus focuses on dish and menu descriptions and encourages critical reflection on dish and menu composition.

Each unit begins with discussion questions and concept introduction exercises to promote critical thought about the book's core concepts. Target language and concepts are then examined via authentic materials such as dialogues, recipes and food reviews. Subsequent exercises encourage learners to apply the book's target language in various situations. The book's concepts are then further explored through a food for thought reading and discussion exercise. Each unit concludes with exercises for checking understanding of the unit's key language.

# Contents

# Part 1

# Back of House Skills

## — Recipes and Kitchen Basics

# Part 1
## *Back of House Skills* —Recipes and Kitchen Basics

Culinary Arts professionals and students must develop many skills. They must learn kitchen safety and food safety standards. They should learn traditional and modern preparation techniques, and how to handle and prepare ingredients. They should look at classic recipes and study how food has changed so that they can see where food is going. They must do all of these things, while learning to handle the many other things that come up in the **back of house** in a restaurant or hotel kitchen. And, they should do so while balancing the precision needed for consistency in restaurants, and their personal creativity as chefs.

This section focuses on English language recipe reading and writing, so that culinary arts professionals can increase the range of sources on which they develop their work. Every word within a recipe has important meaning for cooking processes. So, this section takes a step by step knowledge building approach. Part 1 begins with warm-up exercises to get started with thinking about ingredients and kitchenware, and then looks at the recipe details needed to cook with precision.

## Discussion

To start with, take a look at a recipe in your local language. Think about the kind of language that you need to be able to read or write a recipe in English as you answer or discuss the following questions:

- Can you already explain the ingredients that you would need to prepare the dish?

- Can you explain the kitchenware, equipment, appliances, tools or utensils that you would need to prepare the dish?

- Can you explain the instructions (preparation techniques or other cooking methods)?

- What kind of details need to be explained to follow the recipe precisely?

*Introducing*
*Concepts*

# Components of a Recipe

Here is a short exercise that will make this section's focus clearer and illustrate how important each piece of language in a recipe is. Identify the language in this set of instructions by thinking about which of these categories each piece most closely relates to:

a. Ingredients

b. Kitchenware (Appliances, Equipment, Tools and Utensils)

c. Preparation Techniques/Method Verbs

d. Cooking Process Details

**Simple**
**Chicken**
**Soup**

1. Cut and separate a chicken.

2. Dice the celery.

3. Peel and slice carrots into ¼ in. slices.

4. Roughly chop an onion.

5. Add chicken to a pot of cold water. Bring to a boil.

6. Reduce heat when pot begins to boil.

7. Add the vegetables. Season with salt and pepper.

8. Simmer for 45 minutes. Stir occasionally.

• Is there much unmentioned kitchenware in the recipe? What items do the methods imply?

# Unit 1  Ingredients, Measurements and Quantities

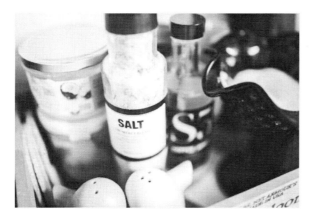

Ingredients are one of the most important parts of learning English for the culinary arts. Ingredients, along with preparation and cooking vocabulary (as well as the descriptive details that explain cooking processes) make up the basis for reading and writing recipes[1].

However, ingredients themselves are much more than words in recipes. Ingredients are the basis on which cooks and chefs develop their work. They determine what chefs can cook and they determine the types of menus that chefs design. Ingredient quality determines how ingredients are used and whether or not chefs select particular ingredients for use. Such is perhaps why Dornenburg and Page (1996) suggest that through ingredient selection and ingredient pairing in dishes, culinary work becomes a 'Culinary Art'.

Talking about ingredients in terms of measurements and quantities is important, too. Making sense of informal and exact measurements is important where cooking needs to be consistent. Talking about and understanding quantities is also important for stocking kitchens and sharing details about recipes with others. This section thus also looks a little bit at the language of quantities and measurements.

---

[1] We will look at how ingredient lists are formed more in Unit 3. For now, the focus is on the ingredients themselves.

# Discussion

 Ingredients are one of the most important things to learn. But, ingredient vocabulary is basically limitless. So, it's up to you to learn the words that you'll use most, and the ingredients most important for the cuisine that you're most interested in. Before starting the exercises, answer or discuss the following questions:

· Generally speaking, how do ingredients vary between cuisines?

· What kind of ingredients do you see as universal between the cuisines that you're interested in? Why do you think some ingredients are universally used?

· How important is it for measurements to be exact when cooking? How important is it when baking? Are there times when it is more or less important?

## Ingredients

There is a lot of language used when talking about ingredients. Often, ingredients are talked about in in categorical terms or as types of ingredients. Some ingredient categories are large and some are small. And, some ingredients belong to many different categories.

Familiar categories include things like Meat, Vegetables, Fruit, Dairy, Grains and Cereals, and Seafood. Some larger categories include these categories. For example, Proteins and Produce are other ways that people usually refer to meats, vegetables and fruit. Sometimes meats are specified into categories such as Red Meat, White Meat and Poultry. Seafood is often separated into smaller categories, among them Fish and Shellfish. Produce like Vegetables and Fruit are separated into their many specific categories—leafy vegetables and citrus fruit and many others. Some other ways people talk about ingredients include calling different items Starches (like rice or potatoes), and Seasonings like Herbs and Spices. Occasionally, people talk about 'Groceries' like Condiments, Sauces and Prepared Foods.

When reading recipes, there are other ways ingredients are categorized. You may see things like 'dry ingredients' (like flour), 'liquid ingredients' and 'wet ingredients' (like sauces or water). Although there are definitely other ways that people talk about ingredients, these should be enough for you to get through the exercises here and for general working purposes.

Before continuing to the exercises, think of ingredients that match these categories and category combinations. If you need more practice with specific ingredient types, refer to the Self-Study Resources section.

- What is an ingredient that is a red meat and a protein?

- What is an ingredient that is a vegetable and a starch?

- What is dry ingredient?

- What is a wet or liquid ingredient?

- What is a protein that is not a meat?

- What is a grain or cereal that is also a starch?

- What is an ingredient that is a white meat and poultry?

· What is an example of **seafood** that is not a **shellfish**?


· What is a food item that is a **condiment** and a **sauce**?


· What is an ingredient that is an **herb** and a **seasoning**?


· What is an example of a **prepared food grocery** that is a **starch**?


· What is an example of **produce** that is a **leafy vegetable**?


· What is an example of a **fruit** that is not **citrus**?


· What is an example of a **dairy** ingredient that is a **liquid**?

## Common Ingredients in Korean Dishes

With the popularity of Korean restaurants abroad, the spread of Korean pop culture, and Hansik globalization campaigns (see: Jeon 2012), many people are now familiar with and enjoy **Korean cuisine**. And, many people even try to work with Korean ingredients and prepare Korean cuisine at home. So, to start your studies, read and fill in the ingredient chart. Think about:

**1)** Ingredients that Korean cuisine often uses

**2)** Dishes that use the ingredients.

| Ingredient Categories | Examples | Foods that use the Ingredients |
|---|---|---|
| **Seafood (Fish and Shellfish)** | Clams | |
| | | |
| | | |
| | | |
| **Fruit** | Pear | |
| | | |
| | | |
| | | |
| **Meats** | Pork | |
| | | |
| | | |
| **Vegetables** | Bracken Fiddlehead | |
| | | |
| | | |

## Aromatics, Seasonings and Spices in Korean Dishes

The aromatics, seasonings and spices that cuisines use are among the most important ingredients to learn. That is where a lot of flavor comes from. According to the Institute of Traditional Korean Food (2007), the following are among the most common sources of flavor in Korean cuisine. Some of these are vegetables, but are so common that we don't want to skip them. Identify what these ingredients are and think about some foods that use them.

| Ingredient Categories | Ingredient | Foods that use the Ingredients |
|---|---|---|
| Seasoning | Black Pepper | |
| | Cinnamon | |
| | Mustard | |
| | Red Pepper Powder | |
| | Salt | |
| Sauces and Pastes | Red Pepper Paste | |
| | Soy Sauce | |
| | Soybean Paste | |
| Common Vegetables | Cabbage | |
| | Garlic | |
| | Ginger | |
| | Green Onion | |
| | Pepper | |
| Other Common Ingredients and Groceries | Fermented Seafood | |
| | Oil | |
| | Vinegar | |
| | Sesame Oil | |

• Can you think of any other ingredients that these lists skipped that kitchens serving Korean cuisine must have? Take a few notes below:

## Other Cuisines

Not everyone specializes in Korean cuisine. It's important that your English language study meets your personal needs. So, think about another cuisine that you're interested in studying. Take some notes about the most common ingredients of the following types below.

**Cuisine:**

| Ingredient Type | Common Ingredients |
| --- | --- |
| Proteins | |
| Dairy | |
| Produce | |
| Starches | |
| Sauces and Seasonings | |
| Other Groceries | |

## A **Deserted Island**

An interesting question came out of a survey conducted by Dornenburg and Page (1996). They asked chefs what ingredients they would choose if they could take only ten ingredients to a deserted island. Not every ingredient was the same for every chef, but the most popular responses were:

Salt

Olive Oil

Tomatoes

Greens (Leafy Green Vegetables) or Spinach

Wine or Grapes

Citrus Fruit (e.g. Lime, Lemon and Orange)

Potatoes

Bread or Wheat

Garlic

Pork

Chicken and Eggs

The chefs were able to suggest some creative recipes with the ingredients they chose. Looking at the ten most popular ingredients listed, what foods do you think you could make?

# Your Own Deserted Island

How would your list compare? What ten ingredients would you have if you could use only those ingredients for the rest of your life? Provide a list of ten ingredients and suggest some foods that you could make.

| Ingredient | Example Dishes |
| --- | --- |
| 1. | |
| 2. | |
| 3. | |
| 4. | |
| 5. | |
| 6. | |
| 7. | |
| 8. | |
| 9. | |
| 10. | |

## A Bit on Measurements and Quantities

Just like knowing the ingredients that go into foods, it is important to be able to understand and explain cooking processes and ingredients in exact measurements and quantities. This is especially important where consistency and precision is needed such as in restaurant services.

However, the language of measurements is not always clear or precise. Many recipes go back and forth between weight and volume measurements. And, many recipes use imprecise measurements—some recipe methods will say to add a dash or a pinch of an ingredient (small amounts of dry or liquid ingredients). Other recipes use words like packed (pressed dry ingredients) and rounded spoon measurements (spoons filled beyond their bases). Such variation may be why weight is preferred for precision for many types of recipes (see: Gisslen 2006). And, of course, different recipe sources vary between metric, imperial and US customary units. So, even 'pints', and 'quarts' might not be the amounts that you think. Then there are the ingredients that themselves are different—vegetables for example. Although some recipes use measurements like cups of diced onion or minced celery, other recipes list onions, carrots, celery, or potatoes by size. But what is a 'small', 'medium' or 'large' onion or carrot?

There is also a lot of language for discussing quantities of items. People may talk about having sacks, jars, bottles, packages, or bags of ingredients, which are also specified in terms of volumes and weights. You might hear such language when talking about quantities for large volume cooking, when discussing a kitchen's stock or when restocking a kitchen for service. Then there are the *strange* quantities like a baker's dozen—13 of a baked item.

No matter how precise or imprecise different measurements are, under-standing them is important when following recipes. Measurements are often used both as abbreviations and in full words in speech. Like many recipe sources, the recipes in this book go back and forth between weight and vol-ume measurements. And, like different recipe sources, Metric, Imperial and US measurements are all present in this book. So, to ensure understanding of the later recipe exercises, look over the abbreviations here and match them with their words.

## Abbreviations

| Pt. | gal. | mL | Tbsp. | 1/3 | Kg | lbs. | ¾ |
|-----|------|-----|-------|------|------|------|-----|
| oz. | ¼ | g. | L | qt. | tsp. | c. | ½ |

## Weight
Gram

Kilogram

Ounce

Pound

## Other Words for Measurements
One third

One half

One quarter

Three quarters

## Volume
Cup

Gallon

Liter

Milliliter

Ounce

Pint

Quart

Tablespoon

Teaspoon

*In Context*    # Identifying Baking Ingredients

Bakers often have to be very precise with recipes. Baking instructions are thus great for practice with reading measurements and studying different ingredients. Read the instructions below. Think about what is being made and take notes of the ingredients and quantities needed.

# A recipe for ... _____

Preheat oven to 180. Cream one and a third cups peanut butter, one half cup butter, two thirds of a cup brown sugar and three quarters of a cup granulated white sugar. Add 2 large eggs, one and three quarters teaspoons baking soda and one teaspoon vanilla. Mix. Add four and one quarter cups instant oatmeal, 12 ounces chocolate chips and one half cup peanuts. Mix until combined. Grease two baking sheets with about a tablespoon of butter. Drop large spoonfuls of dough onto baking sheets. Bake 14 to 16 minutes or until golden brown. Yields 2 dozen large cookies.

**Bartender Training**

Studying cocktail recipes is a good way to familiarize yourself with both formal and informal measurements.  Read the dialogue before answering or discussing the questions on the next page.

| | |
|---|---|
| Al | Hey, Ben. How is your bartender training going? |
| Ben | Not bad. I'm practicing making a cocktail that I can't seem to get right. You did some bartender training in the past, right? How do you make a Margarita on the rocks? |
| Al | I did. That's a famous Mexican drink—everyone has to be able to make a margarita. So, first, fill a cocktail shaker with crushed ice. |
| Ben | I see. What's next? |
| Al | Next, pour in two ounces of tequila. Then add one ounce of orange liqueur. |
| Ben | OK. Orange? |
| Al | Yes. The cocktail has a mix of citrus flavors.  Next, squeeze a fresh lemon into the shaker. You should add about two ounces of lemon juice. |
| Ben | Orange and lemon—that sounds nice. |
| Al | Orange, lemon and lime!  Next, add a dash of lime juice or squeeze half of a lime into the shaker.  Then, you shake it to chill and mix. Then, dip the rim of a glass into lemon juice and salt.  Finally, add some ice cubes to the glass, pour the liquids into the glass and you have a margarita on the rocks. |
| Ben | Salt? |

Al     Salt makes sweet tastes stronger. That will balance the alcohol's bitter taste. We'll talk about that later though.

Ben     OK. What should I garnish this with?

Al     Oh, right. Garnish the margarita with a slice of lime and serve!

· What are Al and Ben making?

· What ingredients are needed for the recipe?

## Stocking for a Special Dinner

Your chef is hosting a Chuseok themed party for 20 of his or her closest friends. They're going to bring in some of the side dishes, but the some of the main dishes are going to be made in house. Your boss also wants you to cost the dishes for the whole party.

Your work will be divided with your team, so pick one dish and cost it. These dishes must be prepared in house:

Galbi Jjim (Braised Beef Short Ribs)

Cod and Kochi Jeon (Cod and Various Skewered Pancakes)

Songpyeon (Sesame, Chestnut and Red Bean Filled Rice Cakes)

Japche (Stir-fried Glass/Starch Noodles)

| Dish: | | |
|---|---|---|
| Ingredient | Quantity | Price |
| | | |
| | | |
| | | |
| | | |
| | | |
| | | |
| | | |
| | | |
| | | |
| | | |
| | | |
| | | |

## Apply It

Imagine for a moment that you are planning a dinner for a dozen people. Plan a menu of any cuisine type and estimate the quantities of ingredients that you will need. Estimate using the quantities discussed in the previous sections.

| Dishes | Estimated Ingredient Quantities Per Person or in Total |
|---|---|
| Dish #1 | |
| Dish #2 | |
| Dish #3 | |

# Food for Thought

Cuisines are characterized by many things. For example, many people describe a cuisine by talking about its famous dishes or the ingredients that it commonly uses. How a cuisine's favorite dishes were invented is complicated. Traditions, beliefs, complicated histories, resources, peoples' tastes, and chefs' best use of the best available ingredients all influence the foods that represent a cuisine.

California cuisine is just like every regional cuisine, but characterizing it is complicated. Like every cuisine, Californian cuisine focuses on peoples' favorite tastes and the best use of the best available ingredients. Many chefs focus on the basics. They like to use fresh fish and seasonal produce to make the best tasting food. And, most chefs try to keep Californian food light because California is a health-first state. However, Californian chefs' favorite tastes have been influenced by foods from many cultures, which makes it difficult to further characterize. California's history that has involved the mixing of many cultures and cuisines from all over the world.

The mix of cultures and cuisines has led to many fusion foods being among Californian cuisine's favorite dishes. For example, California Pizza is an Italian-style dish with toppings like seasonal artichoke and goat cheese, and other favorite flavors like American BBQ, or Thai Peanut Chicken made into pizzas. Other California favorites include sushi rolls with California's fresh avocados. LA style Korean-Mexican fusion tacos are another favorite. These tacos combine Korean and Mexican flavors in a favorite Mexican style.

Some people think that pure cuisines are the best. However, every cuisine is based on chefs using the best available ingredients in the ways that match peoples' favorite tastes. So although Californian cuisine is influenced by many factors, Californian cuisine is pure in the tradition of California. It matches Californians' diverse people with their diverse favorite tastes, using the best available ingredients and resources.

## Questions for Thought

- How would you characterize your local cuisine?

- What foods are famous in different regions in your country?

- Have you seen much change in the ingredients used in your local cuisine or the styles of dishes that people eat?

- Have you seen any new traditions invented?

# Vocabulary from the Exercises

Although each section asks you to decide on the vocabulary most important to you, here is some vocabulary from the exercises that you can study to reinforce what you've learned. Then, check your understanding on the next page.

| General Vocab. | | Recipe Verbs |
|---|---|---|
| Available | Pastes | Add |
| Beliefs | Poultry | Bake |
| Citrus | Produce | Combine |
| Coated | Protein | Cream |
| Cuisine | Pure | Drop |
| Dash | Quantity | Fill |
| Dish | Raw | Garnish |
| Flavor | Region | Grease |
| Fluid | Round | Heat |
| Fresh | Sauces | Mix |
| Fusion | Seasonal | Pour |
| Garnish | Seasoning | Shake |
| Grocery | Softened | Squeeze |
| Heavy | Starch | Stir in |
| History | Taste | |
| Influence | Texture | |
| Liquid | Traditions | |
| Light | Volume | |
| Measurement | Weight | |

## ✓Check your Understanding

Quiz yourself on the vocabulary by reading over the sentences below and choosing the words that fit the sentences best.

1) Spring is one of the best seasons for fresh (produce / pure).

2) This dish is from the southern (seasonal / region).

3) Every cuisine has a complicated (texture / history).

4) Most chefs are influenced by (traditions / fusion).

5) This cuisine has had a lot of (influence / pure) from many other cultures.

6) We have to wait for the butter to be (softened / starches) before we start mixing.

7) Did you order the right (measurement / quantity) to feed this many people?

8) This chicken should be accompanied by a nice (paste / sauce).

9) When the butter is softened, you can (cream / starch) it with the sugar.

10) (Combine / Shake) the dry ingredients in a mixing bowl.

11) (Stir in / grease) the baking sheet before (dropping / round) the dough on it.

12) We should add a (garnish / produce) on the plate to make it more appealing.

13) Most chefs try to use the best ingredients (available / taste).

14) (Combine / Pour) the liquid into the pot.

15) (Drop / Squeeze) the lemon juice.

16) We don't need much—just add a (fill / dash).

17) The cake is already (coated / pour) with chocolate.

18) Why don't you add a little bit more (liquid / paste)? This sauce seems a little bit thick.

19) (Add / Combine) the salt to the mixture.

20) I'd like to eat a (fusion / light) dinner. I had a big lunch.

# Unit 2 Kitchenware, Appliances, Equipment, Tools and Utensils

Kitchenware terms usually pop up when reading recipes. Knowing to use particular items and which appliances, tools, utensils or equipment makes a big difference when following a recipe and on what you can cook. On one hand, knowing whether you have the necessary appliances available when reviewing a recipe affects whether and how you cook certain foods. At the same time, appliances, tools or equipment change the outcomes of your food. Different kitchenware affects the cooking process and kitchenware affects how flavors and textures come from your ingredients (see: Myhrvold, et al. 2011).

Like ingredients, there is a lot of kitchenware vocabulary to learn. This section presents some common items used in the preparation of different cuisines. As you proceed through this section, think about some other kitchenware that isn't mentioned and how and why it is important to your own work.

## Discussion

Think about how the use of different kitchenware affects cooking processes as you discuss or answer the following questions.

- Think about your culinary arts classes or your workplace. What are the most used appliances or other items in the kitchen? What could you not work without?

- How can different kitchenware cause differences when following the same recipes?

- Do different cuisines need different types of kitchenware?

*Warmup*

# Kitchen Tools and their Relationship to Cooking Instructions

Interestingly, and somewhat helpfully, many kitchen tools often share similar words with cooking instructions. Such is not a rule, but here are some examples that can be helpful, and some extra descriptive words that will be helpful when we look at ingredient lists in Unit 3 and for talking about food in Unit 5.

| Kitchenware (Nouns) | Preparation Methods (Verbs) | Descriptive Words (Participle Adjectives) |
| --- | --- | --- |
| Grill | Grill | Grilled |
| Pot / Pan | Boil | Boiled |
| Broiler | Broil | Broiled |
| Fryer | Fry | Fried |
| Knife | Cube | Cubed |
| Knife | Chop | Chopped |
| Grater | Grate | Grated |
| | Brown | Browned |
| Pan | Pan-fry | Pan-fried |
| Roasting Pan | Roast | Roasted |

# A Few Examples...

Look over the example instructions on the next two pages and fill in the sentences using these words:

| | | |
|---|---|---|
| Cutting board | Mixer | Grater |
| Peeler | Ladle | Roasting pan |
| Masher | Rolling pin | Measuring spoons |
| Whisk | | |

· Using a _____, mash the vegetables.      · _____ the batter onto a hot pan.

· Cut the radish on a _____ .      · Roll the dough with a _____ .

· Measure using _____ .

· Roast the vegetables in a _____ .

· _____ the ingredients.

· Peel the apples with a _____ .

· Grate the cheese using a _____ .

· Mix the ingredients using a _____ .

As mentioned, such examples are not universal. The next few pages will illustrate that there is a lot of language needed where cooking process, preparation verbs and kitchenware are concerned. For example, you might:

- *Stir* with a ___wooden spoon___ .

- *Sauté* vegetables in a ___frying pan___ .

- *Turn/Flip* the pancake with a ___spatula___ .

- *Remove* the meats from the grill using ___tongs___ .

# Common Cooking Process and Preparation Verbs

Often kitchenware isn't specified in recipes. Here is a list of common verbs that you'll find when reading recipes. If you were to see these instructions in a recipe, what kinds of kitchenware would you think to use? (Note: not every instruction implies an appliance or tool.)

| Example Instructions | Equipment or Appliances |
|---|---|
| **Add** the broth to the pan. | |
| **Blend** the ingredients. | |
| **Chill** the dough. | |
| **Clean** and **peel** the shrimp. | |
| **Core** the pepper. | |
| **Dip** the chicken in the sauce. | |
| **Grate** the ginger. | |
| **Layer** the cake with icing. | |
| **Melt** butter in a pan. | |
| **Mix** the ingredients thoroughly. | |
| **Pour** the sauce over the vegetables. | |
| **Season** with salt and pepper. | |
| **Seed** the paprika. | |
| **Spread** the sauce evenly. | |
| **Stir** occasionally. | |
| **Turn** / **Flip** the pancakes after 2 minutes. | |

## Prepping to Cook

Think about the following foods. What kitchenware do you need to make each?

### A Loaf of Bread

### Bibimbap

## Pasta with Red Clam Sauce

## Vegetable Cream Soup

## Udon

## Your Knife Set

There are a variety of skills that require knives. For example, you may need to prepare ingredients in these cuts:

| | | |
|---|---|---|
| | Brunoise | Cut |
| | Carve | Dice |
| Chiffonade | Julienne | Slice |
| Chop | Mince | Trim |
| Cube | Peel | *Others...?* |

And, different knives are right for different jobs. How many different knives do you have in your set? What are they? Which knives work best for which types of cuts? Think about that as you fill in the details about your knife set. Then check out the 'cuts' chart on the next page.

| Plain Blades | Granton Blades | Serrated Blades |
|---|---|---|
| | | |

Think about the following knife cuts and slices and the type of knife that you'd need to make each. Then, think about an ingredient appropriate for a particular cut and the type of dish that such is needed in.

| Preparation | Knife | Example Ingredient | Dish |
|---|---|---|---|
| Brunoise | | | |
| Carve | | | |
| Chiffonade | | | |
| Chop | | | |
| Cube | | | |
| Cut | | | |
| Dice | | | |
| Julienne | | | |
| Mince | | | |
| Peel | | | |
| Slice | | | |
| Trim | | | |

*In Context*  **Preparing to Cook**

Read the dialogue before answering or discussing the questions on the next page.

| | |
|---|---|
| Al | Wow you have a pretty full cart there. What are you making? |
| Ben | I'm making chicken noodle soup. |
| Al | Is that hard to make? |
| Ben | Well, it takes some preparation and a lot of different kitchen-ware. First, you have to make egg noodles, so I brought out the mixer. I have measuring cups and spoons, because you have to be precise when making things like noodles. The noodles take flour, a pinch of salt, beaten eggs, milk and butter. You mix these ingredients in the mixer and let it rest. Then, roll the noodles with a rolling pin, slice them with your chef's knife, and let them dry before cooking. |
| Al | Right. What about the soup? |
| Ben | For the soup, you need a large stock pot, and I have my usual knife set. I only really need my paring knife, my butcher's knife, my chef's knife, and a good cutting board. I just got this new wooden chopping block to use. |
| Al | Hey, that is nice. |
| Ben | Right. So you have to clean and separate the chicken to make chicken stock—simmer it over low heat on the stove and skim the broth with your ladle as needed. Then you shred the chicken meat. You can shred it by hand or roughly chop it. Then, you have to dice all of the vegetables: onion, celery and |

carrot. You can add potatoes, too, if you like. You also need to mince some garlic, chop some tarragon and parsley leaves.

Al     That sounds like quite a bit of work.

Ben    It is, but sometimes good food takes time.

## Chicken Soup

- Based on the dialogue, what ingredients are needed for the recipe?

- What kitchenware, appliances, equipment or tools are needed for the recipe?

# Recipes

Read through these recipes. Think about the kitchenware (appliances, equipment and tools) that would be needed to follow the instructions.

**Recipe A:**
**Rosemary**
**Focaccia**
(Inspired by
Gisslen 2006)

## Ingredients

650 mL Water

20 g Dry active yeast

1000g Bread or all-purpose flour

30g Salt, separated

10g Sugar

75 mL Olive Oil

3 sprigs chopped fresh Rosemary or 1 tbsp. dry Rosemary

## Instructions

1. Dissolve yeast, 20g salt and sugar in water. Add the water and flour to a mixer. Mix on low for 7-8 minutes or until thoroughly combined.

2. Ferment dough for 1.5 hours at 25 degrees.

3. Roll the dough to about 2cm thickness.

4. Oil a 13×9" oven pan. Add the dough. Stretch the dough to the edges. Brush with olive oil. Press the dough every 6 cm to make small indentations.

5. Sprinkle the dough with rosemary and 10g salt. Let rise for 15-20 minutes.

6. Preheat the oven to 220 degrees.

7. Bake for 20-25 minutes or until golden brown.

## Kitchenware Notes

**Recipe B:
Lemon
Shrimp
Pasta**
(Inspired by
Kittencal N.D.)

## Ingredients

2 lbs. cleaned Shrimp

1 lb. cooked Pasta (of your choice)

½ c. Butter

1 tbsp. Olive oil

3-4 minced Garlic cloves

1 tbsp. grated Lemon peel

½ c. fresh Lemon juice

¼ c. fresh chopped Parsley

¼ c. grated Parmesan cheese

Salt, Pepper to taste

## Methods

1. Melt butter with olive oil in a large pan over medium heat.

2. Add garlic, lemon peel (zest), and lemon juice. Increase heat to medium-high. Cook for 2 minutes, stirring constantly.

3. Reduce heat to medium. Add shrimp. Cook for 5 minutes or until shrimp is cooked.

4. Stir in parsley.

5. Season with salt and pepper.

6. Toss with pasta. Sprinkle with parmesan cheese.

## Kitchenware Notes

**Recipe C:
Mornay
Sauce**
(Inspired by
Ra 2016)

### Ingredients

155g Butter, separated

125g Flour

2 L Milk

75g grated Gruyere cheese

30g grated Parmesan cheese

1 Bay leaf

100g Onion

1 whole Clove

2g Nutmeg

Salt to taste

White pepper to taste

### Directions

1. Melt 125g butter in a pot over low heat.

2. Add flour slowly. Stir constantly. Cool slightly if the mixture begins to bubble.

3. Add the milk slowly. Increase heat to high. Whip the mixture constantly.

4. Reduce heat to a simmer. Add the onion, bay leaf and cloves. Simmer over low heat for 15 minutes. Stir occasionally.

5. Remove or strain the ingredients. Season with salt, pepper and nutmeg.

6. Remove from heat. Add the cheeses and remaining butter. Stir until melted.

### Kitchenware Notes

## Apply it

No two restaurants are the same. But, most restaurant owners have the same costs to think about. They have to think about back of house appliances and installations. They have to think about interior design in the front of house, menu concepts, marketing, permits, payroll and many other things. Starting costs depend on a restaurant's concept and location and many other things. According to Forbes (see: Tice 2013), costs can start from ten million won for a basic restaurant, or about a million won per seat. Fine dining restaurants may cost more than a billion won to open.

• Have you thought about opening your own restaurant? Think about some of the start-up costs and fill in the table below.

| Restaurant Concept | Seats |
|---|---|
|  |  |
|  |  |
|  |  |
|  |  |
| Major Parts to Plan with Estimated Costs |  |
|  |  |
|  |  |
|  |  |
| Total Estimated Costs |  |

## Food for Thought

Kitchenware affects the food that chefs produce. A lot of kitchenware has been made based on what chefs need to enhance cooking processes and make better dishes. The tagine, for example, is a ceramic pot from Morocco. It was designed for slow cooking stews. Its lid is shaped to direct moisture to the bottom of the dish. It is made with ceramic because ceramic is stick resistant when stewing over long times (see: Albala 2011).

Some kitchenware has changed because technology and materials have helped cooks to make food better or make food more easily. Some of these changes are simple. For example, Chinese woks have changed as new metals have become available, but preference for metal type varies by chef and cooking style (see: Myhrvold, et al. 2011). Some of these changes are quite big, too. For example, electronic rice cookers make cooking rice fast and easy compared to stone pots. Sous Vide style vacuum cooking is also relatively new. Sous Vide lets chefs seal their ingredients from air, like sealing ingredients in fat, salt or leaves. But, Sous Vide also lets chefs gently cook at precise temperatures (see: Myhrvold, et al. 2011).

Not everyone likes new technologies. Some people prefer traditional kitchenware and cooking methods. Many restaurants build their concepts around being new or traditional. Using new or traditional cookware and methods is a big part of that. People also have strong beliefs about what is best. That affects their own cooking choices. And, it can affect whether people are open to trying different food and new restaurants.

# Questions for Thought

- Think about your local culture and cuisine. What traditional kitchen items is your local culture or cuisine known for?

- Are there people who use traditional style kitchenware for which more modern appliances, equipment, tools or utensils exist?

- What effects does using traditional kitchenware have on foods when compared to modern appliances, tools or utensils?

- Do you prefer visiting restaurants with new concepts and methods for cooking or those that use traditional approaches?

- Have you seen people's opinions change as new cookware and food styles have become more common?

## Vocabulary from the Exercises

Each section asks you to decide on the vocabulary most important to you, but here is some vocabulary that you can study to reinforce what you've practiced. Then, check your understanding on the next page.

| | | |
|---|---|---|
| Appliances | Cube | Remove |
| Bake | Cut | Sauté |
| Beat | Dice | Seed |
| Blend | Dip | Separate |
| Boil | Drain | Set aside |
| Braise | Fry | Shred |
| Broil | Grate | Simmer |
| Brunoise | Heat | Skim |
| Bunch | Increase / Reduce | Slice |
| By hand | Julienne | Sprinkle |
| Carve | Ladle | Start |
| Chiffonade | Layer | Steam |
| Chill | Low / Medium / High Heat | Strain |
| Chop | Measuring cups | Tender |
| Clean | Measuring spoons | To taste |
| Coat | Mince | Toast |
| Combine | Mix | Toss |
| Core | Peel | Trim |
| Cover | Precise | Until |
| Cream | Puree | Whip |
| Crush | Refrigerate | |

## ✓Check your Understanding

Quiz yourself on the vocabulary by reading over the sentences below and choosing the words that fit the sentences best.

1) The pasta is al dente. I should (drain / combine) the water using my colander.

2) To prepare the pasta, first (boil / broil) some water in a pot.

3) A (paring / serrated) knife works well for slicing bread.

4) (Carve / Chiffonade) the roasted chicken with your chef's knife.

5) (Chill / Heat) the sauce in the refrigerator.

6) (Grate / Shred) the ingredients by hand.

7) Core and (add / remove) the seeds with your paring knife.

8) (Separate / Combine) the vegetables from the stock with a slotted spoon.

9) Puree the ingredients (in the blender / by hand).

10) (Beat / Toss) two eggs using a whisk.

11) (Flip / Toast) the pancakes over using your spatula.

12) (Mince / Peel) a bunch of basil.

13) The pot is boiling over. (Increase / Reduce) heat to medium.

14) (Coat / ladle) the roasting pan with a small amount of oil.

15) (Sprinkle / Crush) the chopped pepper onto the pizza.

16) (Dip / Pour) the pork into the sauce.

17) (Cover / Appliances) the pot with a lid.

18) (Sprinkle / Whip) the cream until it thickens.

19) (Set Aside / Separate) the egg white from the yolk.

20) Remove the bones from the pot and (set aside / strain).

# Unit 3  Precise Recipes and Detailed Instructions

Recipes are short and concise instructions for preparing food. That means that every word within a recipe has important meaning for cooking processes. Because of that, we've had to develop a lot of vocabulary knowledge related to ingredients, kitchenware and cooking process verbs through the first two units. Hopefully, you've had the opportunity to focus on the language most relevant to the cuisine type that you're interested in furthering your study in. Such language should be enough to roughly follow a recipe.

That said, basic cooking instructions may not yield precise results. Often more details are needed, especially where standardization and consistency is important. For example, is recognizing that you should slice vegetables with a knife or a mandolin when making a layered ratatouille enough to know how to make a layered ratatouille? Probably not. Because every word in a recipe has some important meaning to it, details are important to look for in both ingredient lists as well as in recipe methods sections, which this section looks at. This section also presents a simple and easy way for forming your own recipe methods and instructions so that you can share your own creative work.

## Discussion

 Think about the times in which you've had a cooking method or procedure explained to you, or when you've shared cooking methods or procedures with others as you answer or discuss the following questions.

- What kind of details do you need when looking at cooking instructions to follow a recipe precisely?

- How precise are you when explaining cooking methods to others at home? What about at work or in culinary school?

# Details Everywhere!

There are details everywhere in recipes. But, if you know what to look for, recipes are clear and easy to follow. You'll see **participle adjectives** in recipes' '**ingredients**' sections in almost every English language recipe, including those in this book. Participle adjectives are the adjective forms of **verbs**. Not only do they help you when reading recipes, they can save you time when you're writing your own recipes. Remember this, too, because it is also helpful when talking about ingredients and food (Unit 5).

Here are some examples of recipe instructions and participle adjectives:

Peel the carrots. / Peeled carrots

Cook the angel-hair pasta. / Cooked angel-hair pasta.

Grate the cheese. / Grated cheese

Mix the ingredients in a bowl. / Mixed ingredients

Mince the garlic. / Minced garlic

Dice the carrot. / Diced carrot

Chop the onion. / Chopped onion

Grind the pepper. / Ground pepper

Chill the butter. / Chilled butter

Beat the eggs. / Beaten eggs

For more context, look at these ingredients lists. Notice that simple instructions are put in the ingredient list to keep the recipe short and clean. Can you identify where the simple preparation steps are presented as adjectives?

**Candied Nuts and Roasted Vegetables**

### Ingredients

2 large Sweet Potatoes

1 large Carrot

2 cups Pumpkin

½ cup Walnuts

¼ cup Pecans

4 tablespoons Butter

4 tablespoons Brown Sugar

Salt and Pepper to taste

### Ingredients

2 large Sweet Potatoes, peeled and cubed to bite sized pieces

1 large Carrot, cut to ½″ slices

2 cups diced Pumpkin

½ cup chopped Walnuts

¼ cup minced Pecans

4 tablespoons Butter

4 tablespoons Brown Sugar

Salt and Pepper to taste

### Method/Instructions

1. Peel and cube the sweet potatoes to bite sized pieces.
2. Slice the carrot to ½″ pieces.
3. Dice the pumpkin.
4. Chop the walnuts.
5. Mince the pecans.

### Method/Instructions

...

## Fill in the Details

Notice that in this recipe there are eight simple steps that you can cut out from the methods section by using simple adjectives. Go through and fill in the details to simplify the methods section.

Yukejang (Spicy Korean Beef Stew)

### Ingredients

1 lb. Beef brisket

5-6 stalks Green onion

1 c. Bean sprouts

1 c. Radish

5-6 Shiitake mushrooms

1 small Onion

1 c. fresh Bracken fiddlehead

3-4 cloves Garlic

1 ½ Tbsp. Sesame oil

2 ½ Tbsp. Red pepper powder

1 Tbsp. Red pepper oil

2 Tbsp. Soy sauce

2 Eggs

Salt and Pepper to taste

Glass Noodles (Optional)

### Methods/Instructions

1. Slice the green onion.
2. Clean the green bean sprouts.
3. Cut the radish into large pieces.
4. Slice the mushrooms.
5. Roughly chop the onion.
6. Slice the bracken fiddlehead into 2-3 inch strips.
7. Mince the garlic.
8. Whip the eggs.
   ...

### Ingredients

1 lb. Beef brisket

5-6 _____ stalks Green onion

1 c. _____ Bean sprouts

1 c. _____ Radish

5-6 _____ Shiitake mushrooms

1 _____ small Onion

1 c. _____ fresh Bracken fiddlehead

3-4 cloves _____ Garlic

1 ½ Tbsp. Sesame oil

2 ½ Tbsp. Red pepper powder

1 Tbsp. Red pepper oil

2 Tbsp. Soy sauce

Salt and Pepper to taste

2 _____ Eggs

Glass Noodles (Optional)

## More on Ingredient Lists

Here are a few extra notes about organizing an ingredient list with inspiration from Gillingham (2008). Read over these tips and ingredients for an Apple Pie (inspired by Food Network Kitchen 2001). Then complete the exercise on the next page.

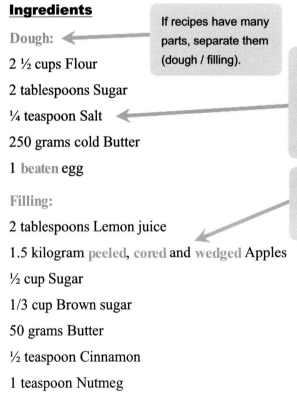

**Ingredients**

Dough:

2 ½ cups Flour

2 tablespoons Sugar

¼ teaspoon Salt

250 grams cold Butter

1 beaten egg

Filling:

2 tablespoons Lemon juice

1.5 kilogram peeled, cored and wedged Apples

½ cup Sugar

1/3 cup Brown sugar

50 grams Butter

½ teaspoon Cinnamon

1 teaspoon Nutmeg

If recipes have many parts, separate them (dough / filling).

List ingredients by **order of use**, or by **importance**. If ingredients are used together, list them by volume (how much).

Put **simple preparation** steps in the ingredient list as participle adjectives.

## Fixing an Ingredient List

Look at the order of these ingredients and the directions below. How would you present the 'ingredients' part of this simple recipe for Spaghetti Marinara?

<table>
<tr><td>

### Ingredients

Salt to taste

Black pepper to taste

4-5 cloves of Garlic

1 large Onion

12 oz. dried Spaghetti

¼ cup Red wine

1 large can crushed or chopped Italian Tomatoes

1 tablespoon dried Oregano

1 bunch fresh Basil

4-5 tablespoons Olive oil

</td><td>

### Ingredients

</td></tr>
</table>

### Preparation/Methods

1. Chop the onion. Mince the garlic. Chop the basil.

2. Heat olive oil in a large pot.

3. Add onion and garlic and sauté. Add the wine and cook on high heat for 3 minutes. Stir in the tomatoes, basil and oregano. Cover and simmer on low heat for 60 minutes, stirring occasionally.

4. Cook spaghetti according to the instructions while the sauce simmers.

5. Season the sauce with salt and pepper. Toss the pasta with sauce and serve.

# Details in Methods and Instructions

Of course, even more critical details are present in a recipe's methods and instructions. Think about these sentence fragments. Which of these recipe process details do they refer to?

| | |
|---|---|
| a. Cooking Time | b. With what kitchenware |
| c. Temperature | d. Other Process Specifics |

## Example Process Details

| | |
|---|---|
| until brown | stirring occasionally |
| until crisp | over medium-high heat |
| for 30 minutes | turning occasionally |
| to 200 degrees | finely |
| using a spatula | roughly |
| with a whisk | at an angle |
| in a large mixing bowl | generously |
| in a 13x9" baking dish | over low heat |
| until tender | until tender |
| in a food processor | stirring constantly |
| coarsely | at high heat |

## More on Details in the Methods and Instructions

Returning to the Apple Pie example, here are a few extra notes about details and organization for the methods and instructions parts of a recipe as suggested by Gillingham (2008).

### Dough

1. Combine flour, sugar and salt in a large bowl. ⟵ Add details about kitchenware.
2. Mix the butter and the dry ingredients.
3. Add the egg. Mix.
4. Press the dough into a ball. Chill for about 1 hour or until firm.

### Filling

1. Add the lemon juice to another bowl.

   Add details about temperatures and cooking time.
2. Toss the apples with the lemon juice, sugar and brown sugar.
3. Melt butter in a pan over medium heat.
4. Add the apples. Cook for 3-4 minutes or until slightly soft.
5. Remove the apples. Add the lemon juice, sugar and brown sugar. Reduce until slightly thickened, stirring constantly. Toss the apples with the reduction and the spices.

### Pie

1. Preheat oven to 190 C.
2. Cut the dough in half. Roll the dough into circles.

   Ovens and stoves are different. Sometimes more details are helpful.
3. Add the dough to the pie pan. Add the filling. Top with the other dough circle. Fold the dough edges. Brush the dough with egg. Sprinkle sugar on the dough. Cut a hole in the top.
4. Bake on a baking sheet for 45 minutes, or until the crust is golden-brown.

# What's missing from these instructions?

Most everyone can cook a steak. Read over these instructions. What kind of details would you need to follow the following example steps? Where and what details would you add to finish the instructions?

### Steak (1 Fillet)

Heat oil in a pan.

Add a whole garlic clove and thyme.

Season the steak.

Cook the steak. Turn the steak and continue cooking.

Top the steak with the garlic and thyme.

Add butter to the pan. Baste the steak.

Remove thyme and garlic. Rest before serving or slicing.

# On Recipe Methods and Instructions Structure...

By now, you will have noticed patterns in recipe sentences through the previous sections. Instructions are quite different from the register (or style) that people use when they speak with each other. Here are a few examples to illustrate the differences. While reading these, think about where different information goes in sentences:

| Requests (Speaking) | Instructions (Imperative) |
| --- | --- |
| | instructions for use |
| **Could you please** open the door? | Open the door. |
| **Would you mind** cutting the cake? | Cut the cake. |
| **Could you** pass the salt? | Pass the salt. |
| **Could you** close the window **please**? | Close the window. |
| **Would you like to** finish your project? | Finish your project. |

Similarly, while the imperative is usually not acceptable for speech, more formal requests are not acceptable in cooking instructions:

| | |
|---|---|
| **Could you** heat oil in a heavy bottomed stock pot? | Heat oil in a heavy bottomed stock pot. |
| **Will you** add onion, garlic and dried red pepper flakes, basil and oregano? | Add onion, garlic and dried red pepper flakes, basil and oregano. |
| **If you could,** sauté for about 3-4 minutes. | Sauté for about 3-4 minutes. |
| **If you don't mind**, season with salt and pepper to taste. | Season with salt and pepper to taste. |

# Writing Recipe Instructions

Knowing content words is enough to be able to read and follow recipes. If writing recipes to share with others, there is a basic pattern that you can follow to make the process easy. The pattern concerns where process details, ingredients, and cooking process and preparation verbs fit in methods sentences. This is not a rule, but for quick recipe recording, follow this sequence to make your own imperative sentences:

Cooking Process Verb  →  Ingredient  →  Process Details

| Process Verb | Ingredient | Process Details |
|---|---|---|
| Roast | the vegetables | at 240 degrees for 40 minutes or until fork-tender. |
| Slice | the chicken | at an angle. |
| Simmer | the sauce | until it thickens, stirring constantly. |
| Mix | the oil and pepper paste | in a mixing bowl. |
| Bake | | in the oven for 40 minutes. |
| Add | the onion. | |
| Toast | | until brown. |
| Mix | the egg, cinnamon and sugar | with a whisk. |
| Combine | the sauce and oil | in a large bowl. |

## In practice

Organize these instructions for a quick and simple breakfast (label the order with numbers, or rewrite the sentences).

Quick
French
Toast
(for Two)

**Ingredients**

4 Slices of bread

1 Egg

¼ cup Milk

1 tsp. Cinnamon

1 tbsp. Butter or oil

Maple Syrup or

Fresh Berries and

Powdered Sugar

1. whisk / in a bowl / egg, cinnamon, milk

2. butter / pan / melt / medium-low heat

3. egg / dip / bread

4. toast / in the pan / the egg-coated bread / until golden brown on both sides

5. *Serve with warm maple syrup or fresh berries and powdered sugar.*

Try these instructions for a brown stock (adapted from Gisslen 2006).

Brown
Stock

### Ingredients

5-6 kg. Veal or beef bones

10-12 L water

### Vegetables

500g Chopped onion

250 g Chopped carrot

250g Chopped celery

500g Tomatoes

### Seasoning Packet

1 bay leaf

¼ tsp. Dried thyme

¼ tsp. Peppercorn

6-8 tsp. Dried parsley

2 Whole garlic cloves

1. Preheat oven to 190C
2. bones / into 8-10 cm. pieces / cut
3. in a roasting pan / put / bones
4. in oven / for one hour / or until browned / roast
5. *Put the bones in a stockpot. Add cold water.*
6. skimming occasionally / simmer / for 4-5 hours
7. *Drain the fat from the roasting pan. Add water. Deglaze the pan.*
8. drippings / add / to the stockpot
9. carrot, celery, onion / brown / in the oven
10. *Add the roasted vegetables, tomatoes, seasoning packet to the stockpot after simmering for 4-5 hours.*
11. *Simmer for 2-3 hour. Skim occasionally.*
12. *Strain the broth. Cool the stock before refrigerating.*

*In Context* **Learning a New Dish**

Read through the dialogue and do or discuss the exercise.

| | |
|---|---|
| Al | Hey, Ben. Are you busy? I've tried to make the new chicken breast dish that chef put on the menu, but I can't quite get it right. |
| Ben | Hey, Al. Let me take a look and a taste... |
| Al | Well? What do you think? |
| Ben | It seems like you're missing some steps. |
| Al | Well, he said to season the chicken with rosemary, salt and pepper. Then, tenderize the chicken a bit to flatten it out. Then, pan-fry it until cooked through. Then, slice tomatoes, cut a chili pepper, add garlic, and sauté. Then, serve. |
| Ben | Right. Well, the first thing that doesn't seem right is that the chicken should be about ¼ inch. So, you need to flatten it a bit. Then, the tomatoes shouldn't just be sliced, they should be quartered. Also, use heirloom tomatoes, not just tomatoes. Plus, the tomatoes are to deglaze the pan when the chicken is almost cooked through. So, just pan fry them, stirring often, for one or two minutes. These tomatoes are overcooked. The garlic is burnt. Try pan roasting whole cloves with the skin on for 4-5 minutes or until they start to soften. Then, peel the whole garlic cloves. The chili pepper should be scored, not just cut. |
| Al | Oh, thanks. OK. Yeah, a few details can make a big difference. |

# Chef's New Chicken Dish

After reading through the dialogue, go back and take note of the ingredients and details needed to cook it properly. Then, try to recreate the recipe methods below.

## Ingredients

## Methods/Instructions

*Exercise*  **Recreating Recipes**

Another way to reinforce your learning and expand your knowledge of cooking instructions in English is through watching chefs work and trying to recreate their recipes. Find an instructional video made by a chef that you like. Take some notes below and then fill in the recipe card on the next page.

*Notes:*

## A recipe for...

**Ingredients:**

**Equipment:**

**Methods/Instructions:**

**How to serve:**

## Food for Thought

Everyone has different tastes when it comes to particular foods. People thus naturally have their own preferences when it comes to cooking different foods, too. Many recipes for the same food taste and are quite different. Some people may add a cooking process to a usual recipe. Others will change the cooking process. For example, some people may grill ingredients when other recipes call for roasting. Many recipes for the same foods will use just a few different ingredients. Some recipes use totally different ingredients.

Sometimes it's hard to put your personal tastes into your work. When working in a professional kitchen, your ability to change menus is limited. And, you must be precise with your cooking so that your dishes are consistent. However, as you rise in the ranks of a kitchen, you may have more options to direct the show, like you can when you cook at home.

## Questions for Thought

- When searching for a recipe for your personal cooking, how do you choose between different recipes for the same foods?

· When you read a recipe, how can you tell what the final dish will be like?

· What is a dish that you like to cook? What has influenced your beliefs about what makes that dish the best?

· Do you or does anyone in your family cook certain foods in ways that are different from popular recipes? How are their styles different and why do they cook the foods in those ways?

## ✓Check your Understanding: Vocabulary Practice

Although each section asks you to decide on the vocabulary most important to you, here is some vocabulary related to cooking methods that you'll need to learn. Read over the cooking methods and ingredients. Write an example dish that matches the cooking method and the ingredients—if there are none, mark the square with a X.

| Cooking Method | Beef | Chicken | Fish | Rice | Vegetables |
|---|---|---|---|---|---|
| Bake | | | | | |
| Boil | | | | | |
| Braise | | | | | |
| Broil | | | | | |
| Fry | | | | | |
| Grill | | | | | |
| *Raw* | | | | | |
| Roast | | | | | |
| Sauté | | | | | |
| Steam | | | | | |
| Stir-fry | | | | | |

# Unit 4 Recipe Wrap-Up Exercises and Projects

Throughout the first three units, you have discovered and explored the language related to the different parts of recipes: ingredients, kitchenware and recipe methods details. Each of these areas of language knowledge is quite large, and each is equally important for cooking precisely. As for ingredients, you should have developed language knowledge relevant to the cuisines that you are most interested in working with. While doing so, you have also hopefully reflected on the effects of different kitchenware on your cooking processes and how specific details can help you to be more precise while working.

To further develop your use and understanding of the concepts introduced in the first three units, this section encourages you to apply each area of knowledge together, just as is needed when reading and writing recipes. After answering or discussing the following questions, work through the exercises, or use them for building projects to further strengthen your skills.

## Discussion

Think about how cuisines vary as well as the importance of specific details when trying to cook with consistency as you answer or discuss the following questions.

- How does your local cuisine differ from other cuisines that you are interested in?

- What do you need to know to create a dish precisely?

- When is precision most important?

- When can you be more experimental than precise?

*Exercise*

## Conceptualizing Vocabulary

Think about the following list of words and try to divide them into the following categories:

M. Measurements               I. Ingredients

K. Kitchen Appliances, Equipment, Tools

V. Cooking Process and Preparation Verbs

| | | |
|---|---|---|
| bake | cup | pour |
| beef | cutting board | refrigerate |
| blend | drain | sauté |
| boil | fish | sesame |
| braise | fry | shred |
| broil | frying pan | shrimp |
| broiler | grater | simmer |
| butter | grill | slice |
| carrot | julienne | soy sauce |
| chef's knife | measuring spoon | soybean paste |
| chicken | melt | steam |
| chill | mince | stir |
| chop | mix | tablespoon |
| combine | mixing bowl | toast |
| cover | onion | whip |
| cream | peel | whisk |

*Exercise*  **Improving Recipes**

Look at this recipe for Bruschetta with Tomato and Basil and take notes about what you would change about its presentation (inspired by Gisslen 2006).

### Ingredients

Salt and Pepper to Taste

2 cloves Garlic

70 milliliters Olive oil

½ tablespoon Balsamic vinegar

500 grams Ripe Tomatoes

8 Fresh Basil leaves

1 Loaf French Bread or Baguette

### Instructions / Methods

1. Blanch tomatoes in hot water. Peel the tomatoes and remove the seeds.
2. Chop the tomatoes.
3. Mince the garlic.
4. Slice or chop the basil.
5. Slice the bread to 15 mm.
6. Combine the garlic, tomatoes, basil, 10 mL olive oil and vinegar in a medium bowl. Season with salt and pepper.
7. Preheat oven to 220 C.
8. Brush the bread with remaining olive oil. Toast for 5 minutes or until brown.
9. Top the bread with the tomato mixture before serving.

*Exercise*  ## Conceptualizing Vocabulary

Think about the following list of words and try to divide them into the following categories:

M. Measurements                I. Ingredients

K. Kitchen Appliances, Equipment, Tools

V. Cooking Process and Preparation Verbs

| | | |
|---|---|---|
| bake | cup | pour |
| beef | cutting board | refrigerate |
| blend | drain | sauté |
| boil | fish | sesame |
| braise | fry | shred |
| broil | frying pan | shrimp |
| broiler | grater | simmer |
| butter | grill | slice |
| carrot | julienne | soy sauce |
| chef's knife | measuring spoon | soybean paste |
| chicken | melt | steam |
| chill | mince | stir |
| chop | mix | tablespoon |
| combine | mixing bowl | toast |
| cover | onion | whip |
| cream | peel | whisk |

*Exercise*   **Improving Recipes**

Look at this recipe for Bruschetta with Tomato and Basil and take notes about what you would change about its presentation (inspired by Gisslen 2006).

### Ingredients

Salt and Pepper to Taste

2 cloves Garlic

70 milliliters Olive oil

½ tablespoon Balsamic vinegar

500 grams Ripe Tomatoes

8 Fresh Basil leaves

1 Loaf French Bread or Baguette

### Instructions / Methods

1. Blanch tomatoes in hot water. Peel the tomatoes and remove the seeds.

2. Chop the tomatoes.

3. Mince the garlic.

4. Slice or chop the basil.

5. Slice the bread to 15 mm.

6. Combine the garlic, tomatoes, basil, 10 mL olive oil and vinegar in a medium bowl. Season with salt and pepper.

7. Preheat oven to 220 C.

8. Brush the bread with remaining olive oil. Toast for 5 minutes or until brown.

9. Top the bread with the tomato mixture before serving.

*Home cooking*

# Similar Dishes, Different Recipes

Read over these home-style recipes for Kim-chi Stew and discuss or answer the following questions. Then, share your own recipe.

• What is similar and what is different between these recipes?

• Which recipe best matches your tastes?

• Are there ingredients or methods that you would change?

Kim-chi
Stew #1
(Inspired by
Kim 2012)

**Ingredients**

4-6 strips of Bacon

½ sliced Onion

2 Tsp. Minced Garlic

½ Tbsp. Red pepper powder

1 C. Chopped fermented Kim-chi

5 oz. canned Tuna

1 ½ C. Water (or Stock)

1 C. Kim-chi juices

200g cubed Tofu

sliced Green onion

Glass noodles

**Method**

1. Fry bacon in a small pot.

2. Stir in onion, garlic and pepper powder. Sauté until onion is soft.

3. Add Kim-chi. Sauté until soft.

4. Add tuna, glass noodles and liquid ingredients. Boil for 10 minutes, stirring occasionally.

5. Add tofu and green onion. Simmer for 3-4 minutes.

**Kim-chi
Stew #2**
(Inspired by
Strange 2013)

## Ingredients

8 Oz. sliced Pork belly

4 C. Fermented Kim-chi

¼ C. Kim-chi Juice

½ sliced Onion

3 diced Green onion stalks

½ Tbsp. Red pepper flakes

½ Tbsp. Garlic

Beef or chicken stock as needed

1 Tbsp. Oil

## Directions

1. Heat oil in a pot. Add onion and cook until soft.

2. Add pork. Sauté until brown.

3. Add red pepper flakes, garlic, Kim-chi and juice. Simmer for up to one hour, or until desired consistency and taste, stirring occasionally. Add stock as needed to moisten.

**Kim-chi
Stew #3**
(Inspired by
Maanchi 2007)

## Ingredients

200 G. Pork belly

4-5 C. chopped Kim-chi

1 Tbsp. Sugar

1 Tbsp. Red pepper flakes

1 Tbsp. Red pepper paste

½ small chopped Onion

2-3 stalks sliced Green onion

200 G. sliced Tofu

2 Tbsp. Sesame Oil

Water

## Methods

1. Boil Kim-chi and Kim-chi juices in a small pot.

2. Add onion, red pepper paste, red pepper powder, sugar, green onion and pork belly.

3. Cover the ingredients with water.

4. Bring to a boil. Then, reduce heat to low and simmer for 20-30 minutes. Stir occasionally.

5. Add tofu. Continue cooking for 5 minutes.

6. Add sesame oil before serving.

**Your Style Kim-chi Stew**

Ingredients:

Equipment:

Methods/Instructions:

How to serve:

*Exercise* **The Budget Chef**

**Situation:** you are preparing dinner. You have 10 points to spend. Look over the ingredient categories and their prices. You may select any specific ingredient from the categories to prepare a creative and balanced recipe that includes a protein, a vegetable, a fruit, and a source of carbohydrates. You should specify the ingredients used. Your kitchen is equipped with common cooking spices, dry essentials, oils, sauces, pastes, condiments, and other liquid ingredients.

Eggs, Tofu/Bean Curd: 1

Red Meat (Beef, Lamb): 4

Pork: 3

Poultry: 3

Fresh Fish: 3 / Shellfish: 4

Roe and Other Seafood: 2

Fruit: 1

Vegetables: 1

Canned or Dry Groceries: 1

Beans, Breads, Grains, Pasta, Rice: 2

*Notes:*

**A recipe for...**

Ingredients:

Equipment:

Methods/Instructions:

How to serve:

*Exercise*    **Recreating Recipes**

Another way to reinforce your learning and to expand your knowledge of cooking instructions in English is through watching chefs work and trying to recreate their recipes. Below is some space in which you can take some notes on a cooking video of your choice. Then, fill in the recipe card provided on the next page.

**A recipe for...**

Ingredients:

Equipment:

Methods/Instructions:

How to serve:

# Front of House Skills
## — Discussing Food and Menus

# Part 2
## *Front of House Skills* —Discussing Food and Menus

Just as everybody eats, every person likes to talk about food, new dishes and new restaurant experiences. For culinary arts professionals, this is especially important—for practical reasons in addition to the obvious personal ones. For

example, if working with an English speaking colleague, describing food and talking about different flavors, flavor profiles, tastes, complements and accompaniments can help you figure out how to best work with dishes on your menu. The same can also help when looking at English language food reviews to examine trends and how people feel about new foods. And, there are some times when you may interact with guests—for example, if you are working in a hotel buffet, or on the restaurant floor you may have to describe dishes to guests with questions. Similarly, being able to describe food can help you introduce your local cuisine to tourists. This section also looks at menu language, because you may have the chance to write your own English language menu in the future, and because menu language can also be helpful if you are studying trends in other restaurant menus.

# Discussion

Think about how you discuss food when out dining with friends, family and colleagues as you answer or talk about the discussion questions below.

· When you tell a friend about a new restaurant, what details do you usually share with them about the food?

· As a chef, when might you interact with guests? What sort of information would you expect to share with a guest about your menu?

· How do you decide how foods, sauces and beverages complement one another?

· What makes a menu easy to read? What details are important to include on menus? How important is it that a menu be consistent in its concept or cuisine?

*Introducing
Concepts*

# Examining Menus

Examine these two example menus then answer or discuss the questions.

### First
Tacos Pescado

Crispy, lightly breaded fried fish, cabbage salad with Pico de Gallo
### Middle
Jangjorim

Soy Sauce Braised Hanoo with a side of fresh Herb Salad
### Main
Persimmon Salad

with Seasonal Vegetables and Sweet Vinaigrette
### Dessert
Salted Chocolates

### First
Hobak Jjuk

### Middle
Sogalbi Gui

### Main
Bibimbap

### Dessert
Dduk and Omija

- Do you know what each of these foods is? How would you introduce these foods if you were discussing them with a friend, colleague or a guest?

- What problems do you see with the menus? How well do these foods match? What would you change about either menu?

- Is there enough detail to know what each dish is?

# Unit 5  Describing Food

Everyone needs to be able to talk about and describe their and other peoples' work, chefs and cooks included. As mentioned, there are many practical reasons why you should be able to do so. For example, you should be able to discuss new restaurants and food trends and discuss new dishes or favorite classics for adding to your own menus with colleagues. You should also be able to examine English language materials and restaurant reviews, so that you can get an idea about what dishes are like and how people like them. Describing food is also important for talking with guests in a restaurant's front of house, or if working on a hotel or other buffet line, especially because people may not be familiar with your cuisine or the creative inventions that you serve. And, describing food is important in casual situations: when dining with colleagues, when introducing new menus and creations to your friends or if a new item is introduced to you while traveling or exploring new areas. This section introduces the English skills required to do so.

## Discussion

 Think about times when you've visited new restaurants or encountered new dishes as you answer or discuss the following questions.

· How do you feel when trying new cuisines or dishes for the first time?

· Think for a moment about when you have encountered a new item on a menu. What kind of details did you want to know about the dish?

· When did you last have a 'bad' meal? What was wrong with it?

# What is it?

When you first see a new menu, you may wonder what the dishes are. However, 'what is it?' is a big question. There are many kinds of details that you could share when explaining what something is. Try to keep it simple. Is it a soup, a stew, a grilled meat dish, a noodle soup, a salad, a rice dish, a pasta dish, a hot pot, or something else? You might also want to know whether a food is a main dish, a side, something to follow a main, dessert, and so on. To illustrate why this is important, look at this example menu for an Italian 5 course meal. Do you know what these dishes are? What are each of these courses?

### Antipasti
*Charcuterie Platter*

### Primi
*Penne di Mais*

### Secondi
*Cotoletta alla Milanese*

### Contorni
*Spinaci Saltati*

### Dolce
*Panna Cotta*

## Traditional or Local Names

As the Italian menu shows, many foods have traditional local names that not everyone knows. Looking at these traditional Korean favorites, what would you say each is?

### A Selection of Korean Favorites...

| | |
|---|---|
| *Bibimbap* | *Japchae* |
| *Bulgogi* | *Pat bingsu* |
| *Galbi* | *Samgyeopsal* |
| *Galbijjim* | *Samgyetang* |
| *Gimbap* | *Tteokbokki* |
| *Jaeyuk Dopbab* | *Tteokgalbi* |

## What's in it and how is it prepared?

Knowing how a food or its ingredients are cooked or prepared can paint a good picture of a dish. To illustrate how a little bit of information can clear up the differences between foods like *galbi* and *galbi jjim*, take a look at these examples. They're both 'rib' dishes, but they're quite different.

Galbi is a Korean **marinated**, **grilled** pork or beef rib dish.

Galbi Jjim is a Korean **braised** pork or beef rib dish with chestnuts, sweet pear and a soy sauce based sauce.

## Describing the Preparation

Just like with our recipe study, participle adjectives can be helpful when describing a dish or a dish's ingredients. Many of the cooking verbs that you've learned can be changed to work in your descriptions. For example, look at these simple directions. You can see which words are nouns (n.) (like kitchenware), which are verbs (v.) and which are adjectives (a.).

### Broiled Steak with Wedged Fried Potatoes

Preheat broiler (n.). Broil (v.) steak, turning after 4 minutes.

Remove steak from broiler (n.) after three minutes. To prepare fried (a.) potatoes for serving with broiled (a.) steak, heat fryer (n.) to 230 degrees. Wedge (v.) the potatoes. Fry (v.) the wedged (a.) potatoes for twelve minutes or until crispy. Season with salt.

Serve the broiled (a.) steak with fried (a.), wedged (a.) potatoes.

## Tossed Salad with Rosemary Parmesan Croutons

For practice, identify the words as: nouns (n.), verbs (v.) or adjectives (a.)

Shred (_____) lettuce. Add the shredded (_____) lettuce to mixing bowl. Slice (_____) tomatoes and other vegetables and add sliced (_____) vegetables to mixing bowl. Chop (_____) bread into bite sized pieces. Grate (_____) Parmesan cheese. Mix (_____) olive oil, rosemary, salt, pepper and grated (_____) Parmesan cheese in a separate bowl. Toss (_____) the chopped (_____) bread in the mixture. Toast (_____) croutons for 2 minutes in the broiler (_____). Turn the bread croutons after 1 minute. Toss (_____) vegetables with sauce and serve tossed (_____) salad with the toasted (_____) croutons and a dressing of your choice.

**Then, you can describe it like this:**

The tossed salad consists of shredded lettuce, sliced vegetables and toasted Parmesan-rosemary croutons.

### Kim-chi Fried Rice

Chop (_____) kimchi and onion. Slice (_____) ham into thin bits. Heat oil in a frying pan and add chopped (_____) kimchi, onion and sliced (_____) ham to the frying pan (_____). Sauté (_____) until cooked and ham begins to brown. Add cooked (_____) rice and a little red pepper paste and mix thoroughly. Season with salt and pepper. Stir-fry (_____) until rice is slightly crispy. Heat oil in another pan and fry (_____) an egg. Plate the fried (_____) rice and top it with the fried (_____) egg.

· **How would you describe this food?**

# Descriptive Language, Tastes, Flavors and Textures

Most people can get an idea of what a food's flavors and textures are like if they know a food's main ingredients and its preparation methods. Sometimes it's just good to talk about how ingredients contribute to a food's overall flavors and texture, or for describing the flavors and textures of whole dishes. But, sometimes it is important to point out textures and flavors. A Korean food like **Naeng-myun** is good example of why it is important to add detail to a description.

## What's missing here?

*Naeng-myun is a traditional Korean noodle dish served with sauce or in broth. It can be eaten as a meal or as an accompaniment to foods like Korean BBQ.*

## More Practice

Think about foods or ingredients that fit the descriptive words below:

| Descriptive Word | Foods/Ingredients | Descriptive Word | Foods/Ingredients |
|---|---|---|---|
| Aromatic / Fragrant | | Hot | |
| Bitter | | Juicy | |
| Bright | | Light | |
| Chewy | | Oily | |
| Cold | | Rich | |
| Creamy | | Salty | |
| Crispy | | Savory | |
| Crunchy | | Soft | |
| Fluffy | | Sour | |
| Fresh | | Spicy | |
| Greasy | | Tender | |
| Hard | | Umami | |

## Something New...

Read over the dialogue before answering or discussing the questions.

Al      Hey, Ben. I tried the new Spanish restaurant last night and it was great.

Ben     Oh really? What's the food like?

Al      Well, we ordered a paella with some sangria.

Ben     I've actually never had Spanish food—I don't know what that is.

Al      Well, sangria is a traditional Spanish wine drink. It has fruit like sliced apples, peaches, pear and berries and a splash of rum. It's not bitter at all—it was sweet, crisp and fresh tasting.

Ben     That sounds good. How about the food?

Al      The paella was really special and the presentation was great. Paella is a traditional Spanish dish, famous in a place called Valencia. Anyway, they served two types: mixed seafood or traditional. We had the seafood paella. We ate a lot but it wasn't heavy. We felt light after eating.

Ben     Great, but what exactly is paella?

Al      Oh, right. It's a rice main dish. It consists of lots of different seafood like whitefish, shrimp, squid and mussels. It's prepared in a large round pan and the rice and seafood simmer together with saffron, paprika and sofrito—a mixture of paprika, garlic, onion and tomatoes reduced in olive oil. The paella had many flavorful ingredients, but it was gentle, savory and fresh. The seafood was tender. I can't wait to go back to this restaurant. I'll call you next time.

Ben     Yeah, let me know—that sounds great.

### Mixed Seafood Paella

· What kind of details did Al share about his dinner?

· What other details would you want to share about a meal?

# Identifying Foods

For a bit more context, read over some familiar Korean food descriptions and identify the foods that are being described.

1. _____ is a savory Korean dish with braised beef short ribs, radish, pear, chestnut and sometimes glass noodles. It's a slowly cooked food that takes a bit of care. The ingredients are simmered until the beef is tender and the sauce begins to thicken. It's savory, slightly sweet and delicious. It is served with rice and it's great around the holidays.

2. _____ is a classic, cold Korean noodle dish with various vegetables like bean sprouts, cucumber and carrots. The ingredients are mixed in a bowl with a spicy chili sauce and then it's topped with a hard-boiled egg. It's spicy but not too spicy, and it has a little bit of sweetness.

3. _____ is a Korean beef stew with shredded beef brisket simmered with vegetables like taro stems, onion, green onion, bean sprouts and gosari (bracken fiddlehead), mushroom, and spicy red pepper oil and powder. It has some glass noodles and egg added at the end. It's spicy, but rich and savory and is best with warm rice on the side.

4. _____ is a Korean stew with a fusion background. It has a milky broth spiced with red pepper paste and it's simmered with vegetables and some salty meats like minced ham and sausage. Some people add sujebi, dumplings and ramen. It has a spicy, robust flavor and it's great with rice.

5. _____ are small Korean dumplings filled with meat or kim-chi, and green onion. Some people add glass noodles or a little tofu. They taste quite savory. They're delicious with a side of soy sauce.

6. _____ is a sweet Korean desert. It consists of shaved ice topped with red beans, sweetened condensed milk, bean powder, different types of chopped fruit and sometimes some jellies and other toppings. It's cold, sweet and great for sharing with friends.

7. _____ is a fantastic, crispy Korean pancake with mung beans, green onion and Kim-chi. The ingredients are blended together and then fried in oil until crispy. It's a little oily but it's great with a fermented rice alcohol drink.

8. _____ is a Korean noodle soup with a clear broth, sliced pumpkin, minced garlic and some seafood like clams. It's great with kim-chi.

## Too Much Information...

Do you think it is possible to share too many details? Look at these examples and think about what you would keep and what you would cross off in a description.

Bibimbap is a savory Korean rice dish that consists of soft steamed rice mixed with a spicy red pepper sauce, some sesame oil, salt, pepper, a runny sunny-side up egg, various vegetables like zucchini, bean sprouts, blanched and seasoned spinach, shiitake mushroom, shredded carrot, bracken fiddlehead (gosari), and topped with sesame seeds. Most of the vegetables are sautéed and it takes a long time to prepare every ingredient. It's delicious with soup like soybean paste stew, but probably not potato cream soup.

## Jaeyuk Bokkum

Jaeyuk Bokkum is a Korean stir-fried pork dish. Many Korean people love this dish and so do spicy food lovers. It consists of stir-fried tender pork belly or pork loin and vegetables like chopped onion, carrot, pepper and green onion. It has a spicy sauce made with red pepper paste, soy sauce, garlic, sesame oil, ginger, sugar, salt and black pepper. The ingredients are usually mixed together before it's cooked in a frying pan. It takes at least 20 minutes to prepare from start to finish. It's stir-fried, so that means you stir it while you fry it. It's usually served with steamed rice.

## Beef Wellington

The origin of Beef Wellington is unclear. There's some great reading that you can do to find out more (see: Hyslop 2013). It is a favorite dish amongst the English. It consists of seared beef tenderloin wrapped with a chopped mushroom, foie gras or pate mixture and then wrapped with flaky pastry. It's then baked in the oven for about 45 minutes or until the beef is cooked through and the pastry is crispy. The Beef Wellington is sliced before serving. Many people enjoy the dish with roasted vegetables or other side dishes. It pairs well with red wine, but not so much with white wine.

## In Practice

 How would you introduce a three course meal of a cuisine that you are interested in? Write a short menu and record how you would describe it to a guest.

What's your menu concept?

| Dish #1 | |
|---|---|
| **Dish #2** | |
| **Dish #3** | |

*In Context*   **Bad Dining Experiences**

Not every meal deserves a nice description. For example, check out the reviews in this dialogue and then answer or discuss the questions.

| | |
|---|---|
| Al | Hey, Ben. Have you tried the new Italian place? |
| Ben | Which one? I tried a new one next to my house and my dinner was terrible. |
| Al | They must be different. I had a great dinner. |
| Ben | What did you have? |
| Al | I had spaghetti and meatballs—the meatballs were really flavorful, tender, juicy and savory and the sauce was bright, thick and a little sweet. The sauce really complemented the meatballs. It came with fresh, crispy but soft garlic bread and sweet, crunchy pickles. I had a glass of dry red wine, too, which really complemented the savory taste of the meatballs. Overall, it was a great dinner. |
| Ben | We definitely ate at different restaurants. I had spaghetti and meatballs, too, and it was terrible. It had dry, overcooked, tasteless meatballs and hard, undercooked spaghetti with a really plain, thin sauce. The whole meal was bland—I couldn't taste anything! What's worse is that it came with cold, soggy and oily garlic bread and old, stale pickles. I had the house wine, too—but it was too sweet. |
| Al | That does sound terrible. I'll call you next time I go to my local place. |
| Ben | Please do! |

### An Italian Dining Experience...

- Did you find any opposite word-pairs in the dialogue?


- Were there any normally positive or 'good sounding' adjectives in the negative description?


- What other factors make a food 'bad'?

## Describing Negative Dining Experiences

Some of the words that we've studied in this section imply nice tasting dishes. But, some can be used to describe something in a negative way.

For example, many people enjoy oily food—maybe fresh, crispy, moist or juicy, tender, salty fried chicken with beer or cola.

Sometimes calling a food oily means that a food is too oily. No one wants to eat chicken that is too oily (or greasy). Even worse, no one wants to eat chicken that is stale, soggy or burnt. Nor would they want to eat chicken that is too salty, tough, or even dry. 'Dry' is a word that might be used to describe a nice wine, but here it means the opposite of moist or juicy. Similarly, all food needs to be cooked—but what about food that is overcooked or undercooked? And, while people like to have hard, crunchy raw carrot, nobody wants to eat a hard, dry piece of old tofu in a spicy braised tofu dish (Dubu-Jorim). And, that spicy braised tofu would be even worse if it was sweet or too salty. Worse yet, every food needs flavor—what about tasteless, plain, or bland braised tofu?

## Apply it

Everyone has had bad experiences with foods that they love. For more practice, think of a food for which you've had both great and terrible meals. Then, describe them each below.

| Food: | |
|---|---|
| Positive Review: | Negative Review: |
| | |

## Food for Thought

Restaurant reviews are serious business for restaurant owners. There are many types of restaurant reviews that people use and many types of critics. Professional critics often publish reviews in newspapers or in restaurant guides. Some people write reviews on review sites or blogs on the internet. Online reviews help people find restaurants that match their tastes and can bring good business, while poor reviews can drive customers away (see: Blanding 2011). Every type of review can improve a restaurant's business. However, they can also be dream crushing, particularly for independent restaurant owners (see: Luca 2011).

Many factors influence these ratings. Some critics from groups like Michelin look at the total restaurant experience: the quality of the dishes, mastery of flavor and technique, how the chef expresses him or herself through their dishes, value for money, and consistency (Michelin Guide Seoul 2016). Many rating systems that we usually find on blogs and internet websites look at service, food quality and value for money.

People are interested in different experiences when choosing restaurants and review systems can be helpful for consumers. They can help people find new neighborhood restaurants and help people choose where to go to for special dining experiences.

## Questions for Thought

- How do you decide what restaurants to eat at?

- How often do you check restaurant reviews? Do you check restaurant reviews for local restaurants or when planning special dining experiences?

- What types of reviews are used in your area? Are there any very prestigious review services used?

- What can restaurateurs do to improve their ratings and reviews?

# Vocabulary from the Exercises

Although most sections ask you to decide on the vocabulary most important to you, here is some vocabulary that you can study to reinforce what you've practiced. Then, check your understanding on the next page.

| | | |
|---|---|---|
| Bland | Greasy | Plain |
| Broth | Heavy | Presentation |
| Complement | Illustrate | Rating |
| Consists of | Juicy | Soggy |
| Dry | Light | Splash |
| Dumpling | Marinated | Stale |
| Experience | Method | Stew |
| Fantastic | Moist | Tasteless |
| Flaky | Oily | Tender |
| Flavor | Old | Thick |
| Flavorful | Old fashioned | Thin |
| Fragrant | Origin | Tough |
| Fresh | Overcooked | Undercooked |
| Gentle | Pairs well with | Various |

## ✓Check your Understanding: **Vocabulary Practice**

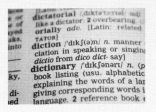

Quiz yourself on the vocabulary by reading over the sentences below and choosing the words that fit the sentences best.

1. The appetizer was too (heavy / light). I'm already full and we haven't started our main dishes!

2. This steak is super (flavorful / tasteless)—salt and pepper with great meat is all you need.

3. The sauce looks a little bit (thick / thin). Try adding a splash of broth to it.

4. They must marinate the pork. It is so (flavorful / tasteless).

5. The sauce was really (gentle / greasy). It let the meat's natural taste come through.

6. The meat is really (tough / tender). I don't even need a knife to cut it.

7. I'm not sure if the food was fresh. It tasted (flavorful / stale).

8. My meal was totally (undercooked / overcooked). It was burnt to a crisp!

9. The (aroma / presentation) was great. It was a beautiful dish.

10. I had a fantastic meal. The wine was a great (complement / flavorful) to the dish.

11. This fried chicken is too (flaky / soggy). The oil must not have been hot enough.

12. That was a great, new presentation style. It's definitely not (rating / old fashioned).

13. The chicken was perfectly cooked—totally (dry / juicy) and flavorful.

14. That beautiful meal (illustrates / various) the chef's good skills.

15. The dish was a little bit too (dry / oily)— way too greasy for me.

16. There's nothing like a delicious, (flaky / stale) pastry for breakfast.

17. I wonder what (method / origin) the chef used for cooking this—I haven't tasted anything like this.

18. The restaurant is getting great (presentation / ratings). It's so popular that it's hard to get a table there.

19. The problem with the dumplings is that they're too (bland / soft). They don't have much flavor.

20. I think they overcooked the dumplings a little bit in the steamer. They're a little bit too (gentle / soft).

**Unit 6** Planning Complements and Accompaniments

Whether it's because of taste, flavor, aroma, textures, or combinations of things that make up flavor profiles, some foods, sauces, and beverages just seem to go together. However, there are many things to think about when planning complements, accompaniments, sauces and beverage pairings for foods.

In some ways, planning meals is a lot like planning the ingredients that go into a dish. You have to think about all of the things that make up the flavors: aromatics and taste, contrast and balance, which is a complicated science (see: Lersch, N.D.). You also have to think about texture matching and contrast. When introducing contrast, you need to make sure that tastes and textures don't clash. And, you don't want to overwhelm the main parts of your dishes. Fortunately, talking about and explaining these things can be simpler than doing the planning itself.

## Discussion

 People don't usually put active thought into the ways that different ingredients, foods, sauces and beverages work together when eating or preparing quick meals.  However, it is important to actively think about how things work together so that your culinary skills stay fresh.  Before starting this section's activities, think about how sauces, side dishes and beverages work together with main dishes as you answer or discuss the following questions.

· Why are some foods commonly eaten together or with particular beverages? What are some examples?

· What is it that makes different flavor profiles match? How can you use this knowledge to plan a dish or a menu?

· Have you ever had a meal whose parts clashed with each other? What was it?

# Enhancing Taste

After thinking about how some foods, beverages and sauces work and don't work together, you can see that there is some enhancement that happens when putting a food together with another food, a beverage or a sauce. According to the Culinary Institute of America (2006), there are a few common things that chefs try for. Taste can be enriched with matching tastes —dishes, beverages or sauces that have similar taste can strengthen flavors. That can give the tastes depth or richness. Taste can also be strengthened with other, different tastes. Finally, sometimes, foods taste totally different but they work together anyway. That is called contrast.

Chocolate is a good example food for how this works. Think about the common pairings below and why they work together. Then, think of some other chocolate combinations that you've tasted that work.

Chocolate and coffee beans

Dark chocolate caramels and salt

Dark chocolate and strawberries

With the chocolate examples, there are few things happening related to balance and enhancement. Add your own thoughts to these explanations if there's anything missing.

### Chocolate and coffee beans

Chocolate and coffee beans both have bitter tastes. The coffee and chocolate's similar bitter tastes give depth (makes the flavor deep) to the bitter flavor. The coffee beans' bitter tastes enhance or strengthen the sweetness of the chocolate.

### Dark chocolate and strawberries

The strawberries' tart or sour taste enhances the chocolate's mild sweetness. The mild sweetness of dark chocolate balances the strawberries' tart taste.

### Dark chocolate caramels and salt

The salt and chocolate example seems strange. But, there's some science that suggests that salt enhances sweetness (see: Yee, et al. 2011). So, the caramel's sweetness is enhanced by the salt. The caramel's sweetness is balanced by the dark chocolate's bitter taste.

## Tastes That Work Together

It's important for chefs to keep their culinary skills fresh so that they can continue to explore the culinary arts. Experts suggest that chefs think about pure tastes and how tastes work together as they work (e.g. Ferriss 2012). Think about the tastes below. Decide which tastes work together in enhancing, contrasting, and balancing relationships and draw connecting lines.

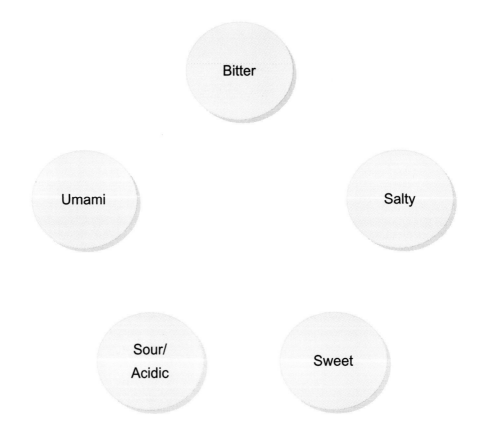

## *In Context*    **Some Foods Just Naturally Seem to Work Together**

Think about the following food pairings. What types of tastes does each food have?  Use the labels as you work through the pairings.

B. Bitter / U. Umami / Sa. Salty / So. Sour / Sw. Sweet

Avocado / Lime

Balsamic Vinegar / Creamy Cheese

Chocolate / Pretzels

Coffee / Donuts

Dark Chocolate / Red Wine

Honey / Gorgonzola Cheese

Lemon / Shellfish

Oil / Vinegar

Pineapple / Ham

Rice / Kim-chi

Spinach / Cheese

Tomato / Mozzarella

White Wine / Cheese

• What are some other examples of foods and sauces or side dishes that work together? How do their tastes work?

# Talk About It

Enhancing taste may be more clear when thinking about dishes. For example, roasted chicken is good with difference sauces. Read through these explanations. Then, suggest another sauce and explain why that works.

**Chicken-stock based cream sauce** complements roasted chicken because it adds richness to the chicken and gives depth to the chicken's savory tastes.

**Balsamic-mustard sauce**'s bright and sour tastes complement roasted chicken because it balances the chicken's rich, oily and savory taste.

- What sauce would you suggest?

## Aroma, Taste, Flavor and Sensations

Taste is helpful for putting foods together. However, taste is not everything. Experts note that taste can be as little as 10% of flavor (Ferriss 2012). Sensations and smell affect flavors, too.

Sensations are the feelings you have when eating. They include things like astringency, like from wine tannins, and spiciness.

Aroma and aromatics affect flavor through smell. Aromatics are ingredients like herbs, vegetables and spices. There are some very common aromatics that add flavor and smell. Onion, carrot, celery (i.e. a Mirepoix), and garlic, ginger and green onion are good examples of these.

Some aromatics are very common between many cuisines like garlic and onion. However, many cuisines use very different aromatics. These may change how foods from different cuisines work together. So, while some flavor matchings might work between cuisines, it's also possible that pairing foods with different cuisine bases may lead to clashing flavors. Another important thing to think about is that preferences for flavor matchings vary among people around the world, just like the aromatics of different cultural and regional cuisines vary (see: Ahn, et al. 2011). So, it may also be important to think about the flavors that your guests like when putting different flavor profiles together.

What are some common aromatics used in the cuisine that you're interested in cooking? Think about the kinds of flavors and sensations that they give and fill in the table below with some examples.

| | Example Ingredients | Flavors / Sensations |
|---|---|---|
| Seasonings | | |
| Sauces, Pastes, Oils | | |
| Vegetables | | |
| Herbs | | |

## An Overwhelming Clash of Flavors

 Having thought about different aromatics from a cuisine that you're interested in, now think about how some aromatics can cause dishes to overwhelm other foods or cause some dishes to clash, as you answer the questions below.

• What types of ingredients and flavors can overwhelm other flavors?

• What types of ingredients and flavors clash with other flavors?

• Are there any aromas or flavors in your local cuisine that would complement another cuisine that you're interested in? What are they?

• Are there any aromatics from other cuisines that clash with your local cuisine?

**New Pairings**

Read through the dialogue and answer or discuss the questions.

| | |
|---|---|
| Al | Hey, Ben. How's sommelier school? |
| Ben | Not bad. We've been talking a lot about food parings lately. We studied steak and wine today. |
| Al | That's easy. Most red wines have dry, full tastes. Red wine complements steak because the full tastes cleanse the palate. They also bring out the full flavors of a fatty steak. The steak does the same thing—the fatty steak flavors complement red wine because they soften the red wine's astringent taste. And, the fattier the cut of steak, the more flavorful wine you need. It's all about wine tannins. |
| Ben | Actually, I had steak with a white wine recently. It was great. |
| Al | Uh... |
| Ben | That's what I thought. See, full flavored white wines can do the same thing. It's just a matter of balancing between the oils and the flavors of the wine. It depends on how the steak is prepared and the flavor profile of the wine. |
| Al | Go on... |
| Ben | Well, for example, a full, bright and acidic white wine complements a fatty steak because it cleanses the palate. The wine cuts through the fatty taste. Contrasting tastes are complements, too. They just enhance taste in a different way. |
| Al | Hmmm... I hadn't thought about that. |

> Ben   Well, not all white wines match well with steak, just like not all red wines match steak. Matching tastes and flavors takes a lot of thought[2].

## Strange Combinations

 Everyone has their own interesting preferences for side dishes, sauces or drinks when eating something that other people might not understand or be familiar with. Think about that as you answer or discuss the following questions.

- What are some unusual flavor combinations that you or someone you know enjoys?

- Are there any interesting combinations that you'd like to try but haven't had the chance to yet? What are they and why do you think they would work well together?

---

2  Discussion based on surveyed chefs and sommeliers (see: Hoffman 2013).

## Complementing Textures

Tastes, aromas and flavors are big, but, they're not everything. To make your food interesting, it may be important to add variety in texture. Just like you may not want to taste the same flavors, you may not want your textures to be repetitive.

But, that is not always the case. As mentioned, some preferences for matching texture and taste are different for different cultures and their cuisines. As an example, I (the author) once had a meal in a very nice Amish community. The Amish are kind and simple farming people that live all over Middle-America. The 'chicken and noodles' dish that I had was also simple and plain. The flavors were rich. But, it was too repetitive for my tastes. As for flavor profiles, it consisted of a savory, cream based chicken sauce with two starches: savory, rich and buttery mashed potatoes and egg noodles. As for the texture, it was a soft, creamy sauce, with soft pasta noodles, and soft mashed potatoes. Another soft, starchy bread was served on the side with rich peanut butter.

The flavor and texture profiles may be suitable for the Amish people. But, I like some contrast in flavor and texture. So, while delicious for some people, the meal did not match my tastes.

## Fixing a Plate

Varying flavors and textures can be done in a few ways. There are also some obvious things to avoid that created problems like those with the chicken and noodles meal. For example, using the same cooking methods like boiling for foods that are served together may cause foods to have similar textures and similar flavor profiles. The same could happen with fully grilled, fried or sautéed meals. Using different classic approaches when preparing ingredients is a simple way to create good texture and flavor variety and balance (see: Myhryold, et al. 2011). Or, if you have flavors profiles in mind that you want to create with certain textures, there are also very scientific methods that you can use (see: Lersch 2010).

Is there anything that you would change about these meals to add some texture, flavor or color variety? Are there any flavors that might be overwhelming that you'd like to change? Read through the examples. Suggest some foods that would provide variety or balance. Cross out the foods that you'd like to replace. Then explain what tastes or flavors the added foods add.

### For example

| Original Combination:<br>~~Egg Noodles~~, Mashed Potatoes, Chicken Cream Sauce and ~~Bread~~ | Foods to Add:<br>Grilled Vegetable Salad with Mustard Vinaigrette |
| --- | --- |
| Explanation:<br>The salad with mustard vinaigrette **complements** the chicken dish because the salad's sour, fresh and slightly bitter grilled taste **balance** the chicken and potatoes' rich tastes. It is also refreshing. The salad's crispy texture and grilled vegetables' firm texture **give variety** to the chicken and potatoes' soft textures. The vegetables also give some **color** to the plate. | |

| Original Combination:<br>Sautéed Mushrooms, Steak, Mashed Potatoes, Béarnaise Sauce, Creamed Corn with Butter | Foods to Add: |
|---|---|
| **Explanation:** | |

| Original Combination:<br>Cream Sauce Penne Pasta, Garlic Bread, White Bread with Butter, Buttered Grilled Vegetables | Foods to Add: |
|---|---|
| **Explanation:** | |

## A mismatched meal that you had recently...

| Original Combination: | Foods to Add: |
|---|---|
| **Explanation:** | |

## Apply It

In addition to these taste, flavor and texture factors, color and other considerations are important parts of putting a plate together. Form a balanced plate below and then explain your choices on the next page.

| What's on the plate? | What's in the glass? |
|---|---|

**Explanation:**

## Food for Thought

Wine is becoming more and more popular in Korea. Some people think that this is because of the global dietary culture accompanying globalization, and because people have learned about red wine's health benefits (Oh 2015).

However, wine is far from the main alcoholic beverage consumed in Korea. In 2013, wine sales were just 4.6% of alcoholic beverage sales; a USDA report says that this is because people don't know much about wine, and because wine is considered a premium product because of high import prices (Oh 2015).

Wine's consumption has had further challenges in Korea. Korean food is usually served with many different side dishes. As a result, there are many flavor and taste combinations served in one meal. That makes pairing wine with Korean cuisine difficult because of the different flavors and tastes served together. The same can be said about Korean cuisine's strong flavors, which can overwhelm or clash with wines. Many people thus believe that wine does not match with Korean food.

Some prominent food and wine journalists, however, disagree. Daley (2006) as well as others (e.g. Zimmerman 2015) suggest that refreshing wines with contrasting flavors like crisp whites or sweet wines work well with Korean cuisine's flavors. Such wines may also work better with the many flavors served in Korean meals, as compared to heavy, tannic and astringent wines, which they say are difficult to pair with Korean cuisine because the flavors may overwhelm each other (see: Daley 2006).

## Questions for Thought

- What types of cuisines have you tasted wine with? Did they match well?

- What kinds of flavor or tastes do different types of wine work well with? What types of flavors does wine clash with?

- What wine making processes are you familiar with? How do those processes affect the wine?

- What types of beverages are best suited for Korean cuisine? Explain your choices.

# Vocabulary from the Exercises

Although most sections ask you to decide on the vocabulary most important to you, here is some vocabulary that you can study to reinforce what you've learned. After reviewing the vocabulary, check your understanding on the next page.

| | | |
|---|---|---|
| Accompaniment | Desired | Plain |
| Acidic | Dietary culture | Provide |
| Aroma | Dry | Refreshing |
| Aromatics | Enhance | Repetitive |
| Astringency | Enrich | Rich |
| Balance | Fatty | Sensations |
| Beverage | Flavor | Soften |
| Bitter / Bitterness | Flavor profile | Sommelier |
| Bright | Full flavored | Spice |
| Buttery | Health benefits | Starch |
| Clash | Heavy | Strengthen |
| Cleanse | Herbs | Suitable |
| Complement | Import prices | Sweet / Sweetness |
| Consist of | Match / Matching | Tart / Tartness |
| Consume | Modify | Taste |
| Contrast | Needs | Variety |
| Crisp | Overwhelm | Vary |
| Cut through | Pair / Pairing | Wine tannins / Tannic |
| Deep / depth | Palate | |

## ✓Check your Understanding

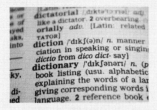

Quiz yourself on the vocabulary by reading over the sentences below and choosing the words that fit the sentences best.

1. The sauce seems too acidic. It (clashes / matches) with our main ingredients.

2. If you want to add some (contrast / depth), match it with a similarly rich sauce.

3. I think we need to modify the recipe. It doesn't (satisfy / suitable) our guests' tastes.

4. Those aromatics are way too strong. They are going to (overwhelm / soften) the natural flavors.

5. Herbs, spices and some vegetables are good examples of (aromatics / astringency).

6. You should pair more fatty beef with (full flavored / soft) wine.

7. A bright, contrasting flavor can help to (cleanse / flavor) the palate from oily tastes.

8. We want to try something with a bright taste to (contrast / clash) with the umami.

9. There are a lot of health benefits to eating (a variety of / repetitive) vegetables. That's why the local dietary culture is so great.

10. We need to plan another colorful (accompaniment / taste) to this meal. I don't think the dish looks balanced enough.

11. I've consumed too many (herbs / starches) lately. I need to cut down on bread.

12. The acidic taste really cuts through the buttery flavors, providing nice contrast. My palate feels totally (cleansed / fatty).

13. That beer was (refreshing / overwhelming) after all of the oily fried chicken.

14. These ingredients provide a lot of different sensations. I think we need to modify the recipe and cut down on aromatics. Some flavors might (balance / overwhelm) the main ingredients.

15. A little bit of rich cream might enrich the flavor profile. I think it could add a tiny bit of sweetness and (depth / tartness).

16. A dry beverage can really (acidic / cleanse) the palate.

17. That sommelier knows a lot about wine. She recommended a great wine to go with a food that I never thought would (clash / match) with wine.

18. These flavor profiles work well together. You made a good choice of (accompaniments / suitable) for the main dish.

19. That wine is too tannic for the food. I think we need to find something more (deep / suitable).

20. The spicy aromatics added a great (enrich / sensation) that matched well with each dish!

# Unit 7 Composing Menus

There are many things to think about when composing a menu. And, there are many different types of menus that you might have to create. You may have to plan a one-time **course dinner**, a **daily menu**, **standing options** on a menu, or a **buffet section's offerings**. You may have **special ingredients** that you want to highlight for a special menu, for a new **buffet menu**, a **rotating menu**, or a **seasonal menu**. You may have to plan a **standing menu** with many options for **a la carte** ordering.

Many things affect how menus are designed. Restaurant concept, the type of service, target clientele, price points, what the kitchen can cook, and the visual design of the menu of itself—whether it's one page, separated by course of by theme or even whether your menu needs pictures all affect menus (see: Garvey, et al. 2011). For our purposes, we want to focus on the **language** of a menu. In doing so, we'll also talk a little bit about **menu composition**.

# Discussion

 There are many different types of menus that restaurants plan. Think about the different types of menus in different types of restaurants that you've visited as you answer or discuss the following questions.

- How much time do you spend reading a menu when ordering? How much time does it take to read a good menu?

- How do menus vary between the **formal** restaurants that you've eaten at and **local** or **casual** restaurants?

- Are menus at restaurants that serve other cultural cuisines different from those that serve your local cuisine?

- When restaurants have **special offerings**, how do they present the **details** of the offerings on their menus?

- Have you ever been to a restaurant whose menu had foods that didn't seem to have a consistent theme or continuity? What was the food like?

**What's on the Menu?**

Every restaurant has its own characteristics. What's on the menu depends on many different things. These may be the restaurant's type of cuisine or service style. Service may consist of a single plate ordered a la carte. Service may consist of many dishes served at the same time. Service may be table d'hote or with fixed menus. And, service may consist of many courses over a few hours. Restaurant service levels are different. Service ranges from informal to formal and that, along with the chef's choices and types of cuisines offered affect how things are organized (see: Dahmer and Kahl 2009).

One thing that many menus do have in common is categorization. We are familiar with many words like:

Appetizers / Aperitifs / Starters / Hors d'oeurves / Soup / Salad /
Entrées / Main courses / Entremets / Removes / Cold Dishes /
Hot Dishes / Proteins / Fish Courses / Meat Courses / Sides / Cheese / Sweets
/ Coffee / Desserts / Beverages / Wine / Alcoholic Beverages

Organization could mean courses. It could mean serving order. It could also mean type of dish: cold dishes, hot dishes, soups, seafood dishes, salads, vegetables, starches, proteins, poultry, and red or white meats. Buffets could be separated by section: hot section, cold section, cuisine type, part of the course (e.g. dessert section) and so on.

### Menu Exercise

Whatever the restaurant concept, menu styles are different. Not every course type is offered in every service setting. There may be more or fewer parts. And, they may be served in any order the chef decides. It's important for you to be familiar with the menus that are most important to the cuisines you are interested in.

Think about these questions while you fill in the chart:

What is an example of a local course menu? What types of dishes are served in each course? How does the local style compare to course menus of another cuisine that you are interested in?

| | | Parts of a Usual Meal | Example Dishes |
|---|---|---|---|
| Local Cuisine | Formal | | |
| | Informal / Casual | | |
| Another Cuisine | Formal | | |
| | Informal / Casual | | |

## What Dishes are on the Menu?

Course menus, a la carte dining menus and buffet lineups are different. But, there are similar principles between them. Dornenburg and Page (1996) surveyed a number of accomplished chefs about how they design their menus. They found that the feature that impacts chefs' choices in menu design the most is...

Season and Market Availability

In other words, chefs like to use the best available ingredients. That might not change a menu completely. But, it is hard to find a restaurant that doesn't offer a special theme menu when seasonal ingredients become available. For example:

Early spring strawberry pastries in a bakery

Late fall and early winter crab legs in a hotel buffet

Fall and winter pears or winter tangerines, and so on...

• What are some seasonal ingredients (seafood, fruits and vegetables) that influence the cuisine that you're most interested in? What are some good dishes that show the **ingredient's quality**?

| Availability | Ingredient | Example Dishes |
| --- | --- | --- |
|  |  |  |
|  |  |  |
|  |  |  |
|  |  |  |
|  |  |  |
|  |  |  |
|  |  |  |
|  |  |  |
|  |  |  |

# Excite the Palate

Now that you've thought about some ingredients and dishes, you have to think about how they would be best presented on a menu. As Dornenburg and Page (1996) suggest, menu language can be used to increase expectations and excite the palate. That can be for tasting menus in fine dining restaurants, casual dining menus, or for a description of a food on a buffet. What you want to do is to use language to paint a picture of the food. In other words, just like food can look appetizing (or delicious), it can sound appetizing. Garvey, et al. (2011) suggest this can also be done to promote sales. Menus also need balance between enough and too much information. Before we get to the balancing, the next few pages contain examples that will illustrate the aforementioned experts' suggestions for menu writing.

- Before looking at the things that the experts suggest, what do you think a menu could include that could excite the palate?

## Say How the Ingredients Are Special

Some types of ingredients are well-known as being high quality. Some places are known for producing special quality ingredients. These are not only great selling points, but can give guests ideas about the types of flavors that they can expect with certain sources or qualities of ingredients. For menus, if an ingredient is sourced from a special place or high quality, it's great to say so.

Pork vs. Jeju Black Pork

Steak vs. USDA Prime Steak

Beef vs. Hoengseong 1++ Beef

Salmon vs. Alaskan Salmon

Tuna vs. Atlantic Bluefin Tuna

Lobster vs. Maine Lobster

Pear vs. Naju Pear

Citrus vs. Jeju Citrus

Ham vs. Iberian Ham

And so on...

## Say How the Ingredients Are Unique or have Special Qualities

Are the ingredients unique? Are the foods specially made or are the ingredients specially selected? Is there any special process related to how the ingredients are made? It's fine to say so.

Beef vs. Dry-Aged Beef

Chicken vs. Free-Range Chicken

Mixed Greens vs. Organic Mixed Greens

Broth vs. Traditional Korean Broth

Tomatoes vs. Select Tomatoes

Pastries vs. Homemade Pastries

Cheese vs. Aged Cheese

Strawberries vs. Seasonal Strawberries

Eggs vs. Farm Fresh Eggs

Mushrooms vs. Wild Mushrooms

And so on...

## Mention the Tastes, Flavors or Textures

Do textures or flavors vary between how the ingredients are usually prepared? Is there something special about an ingredient's texture? Is a texture or taste going to make the dish sound more delicious? Go ahead and say so.

Vinaigrette vs. Sweet Vinaigrette

Dressing vs. Warm Dressing

Rice cake vs. Soft or Crisp Rice Cake

Cucumber vs. Crisp Cucumber Slices

Chocolate cake or Spiced Chocolate Cake

Pastry vs. Flaky Pastry

Oysters vs. Chilled Oysters

Beef vs. Tender Beef

Sauce vs. Spicy Sauce

Onions vs. Sweet Onions

And so on...

## Preparation and Cooking Methods

Is the ingredient cooked in a lot of different ways? Do you cook it in a special way? Does the name of the food not explain how it's cooked? Is there a special way that it's sliced or prepared? It's OK to say how.

Beef Ribs vs. Braised Beef Ribs

Scallops vs. Pan-Seared Scallops

Vegetables vs. Roasted Vegetables

Pizza vs. Wood-fired Pizza

Chicken vs. Rotisserie Grilled Chicken

Tenderloin vs. Grilled Tenderloin

Brisket vs. Smoked Brisket

Prawns vs. Sautéed Prawns

Potatoes vs. Wedged Potatoes

Carrots vs. Glazed Carrots

Yams vs. Candied Yams

Potatoes vs. Scalloped Potatoes

Coconut vs. Toasted Coconut

Chicken vs. Lightly Breaded Chicken

And so on...

## Premium Ingredients

- Before looking at whole foods and menus, think about these ingredients or parts of foods—what are some words that you would use to describe them 'deliciously'?

| Ingredients | In a dish?<br>If so, what? | Example Adjectives |
|---|---|---|
| Cheese | | |
| Tuna | | |
| Tangerines | | |
| Peaches | | |
| Beef | | |
| Salmon | | |
| Peppers | | |
| Mixed Greens | | |
| Pork | | |
| Broth | | |

**Menus**

For more practice, read through the following menus and identify the language used to 'excite the palate' or paint pictures of the dishes.

**Menu 1:**
**At an**
**Italian**
**Restaurant**

## Antipasti

### Funghi Fritti

Select fried mushroom caps

### Minestrone

Traditional Italian vegetable broth

### Bruschetta Al Pomodoro

Hot garlic bread with fresh chopped tomatoes,

finished with virgin olive oil and fresh basil

### Insalata Caprese con Rucola

Fresh baby mozzarella, sliced tomatoes drizzled with

virgin olive oil and fresh basil leaves and served on a bed of salad

## Secondi

### Penne Ariabbiata

Spicy tomato sauce, cooked with fresh chilies and basil leaves

### Vitello Funghetto

Pan fried veal with a rich wild mushroom and white wine cream sauce

### Pollo Romagna

Tender chicken breast wrapped in smoked prosciutto, simmered in a tomato

and fresh basil sauce and topped with aged Italian cheeses,

served with fresh market vegetables

**Menu 2:
At a
Steak
House**

## Appetizers

### French Onion Soup

Baked with Creamy Gruyere and Aged Parmesan

### Pork Belly

Crispy, Pan-Seared Pork Belly with Cherry and Sweet Onion Reduction

### Mussels

Sautéed Mussels with Fresh Garlic, Oven Roasted Tomatoes, White Wine

## Mains

### Seared Tuna

with Fresh Vegetable Salad and Spicy Mustard-Vinaigrette

### Roasted Chicken

Wood-Fired Chicken with Olive oil, Garlic, and Rosemary

## Steaks

### Filet Mignon

1+ Hoengseong

### Ribeye

Prime, Dry-aged

### Ribeye

Prime, Bone-In

### Porterhouse

Certified Angus

### New York Strip

Wagyu

Menu 3:
At a
French
Restaurant

## Poultry

### Canard a la Grenade

Roasted Duck Breast, Sweet Pomegranate sauce

### Coq au Vin

Chicken Braised with Red wine, Bacon, Organic Mushrooms and Onion

## Seafood

### Noix de Saint Jacques au Champagne

Pan-Seared scallops with Fresh Artichoke and Cream Sauce

### Saumon Tout Simple

Grilled Salmon with Asparagus and Light Citrus Sauce

### Escargots

Pan-roasted Snails with Organic Garlic Country Butter

## Beef

### Steak au Poivre, Frites

Prime Hoingsang Strip Steak Coated with Black Peppercorn,

Crispy Fried Gangwon Potatoes

### Filet de Boeuf, Béarnaise

Grilled Beef Tenderloin with Béarnaise Sauce

## A Note on Details

Details are not just important for exciting the palate. You do not want to surprise your guests by not giving them enough information. This is especially important when traditional names are used, like with the menus from the previous exercises. You also do not want your menu to need study—reading a menu should be fast.

Adding specifics is simple. What are the main ingredients? Mention them first or put details like those in the name. For example:

| Roasted Potatoes | A Vegetable |
|---|---|
| Browned Butter and Shallots | Roasted Potatoes with Brown Butter and Shallots |
| Tenderloin with Sautéed Mushrooms | Steak |
| Hanoo, Wild Mushroom | Hanoo Tenderloin with Sautéed Wild Mushrooms |
| Candied Walnut Gorgonzola Salad | Salad |
| Fresh Tomato, Crisp Red Onion, Herb Toasted Croutons and Raspberry Vinaigrette | Rich Gorgonzola, Candied Walnuts, Fresh Tomato, Crisp Red Onion, Herb Toasted Croutons and Raspberry Vinaigrette |

With traditional names, you may have to provide detail. But, there's such a thing as too much information. Menu reading should be fast!

| Bibimbap | Bibimbap |
|---|---|
| Traditional Korean mixed rice with organic vegetables, minced Hanoo beef, spicy red pepper sauce, freshly pressed sesame oil and a rich sunny-side up egg | Traditional Korean Mixed Rice with minced Hanoo, organic Spinach, crispy Bean Sprouts, Gosari, fresh Carrot, savory Onion, Zucchini, Shiitake Mushrooms, Spicy Red Pepper Sauce, freshly pressed Sesame Oil, topped with a Sunny-side up Egg |

Although you have to avoid 'too much information', some specific details are important to include.  For example:

| 'Sauce' | Demi-glace, Reduction, Mornay, Hollandaise, Vinaigrette, etc. |
|---|---|
| 'Herbs' | Rosemary, Thyme, etc. |
| 'Vegetables' | Turnips and Potatoes, Carrot and Peas, etc. |
| 'Salad' | Lentil Salad, Bean Salad, Spinach Salad, Arugula Salad, Mixed Greens |

Finally, some strong flavors and aromatics should be mentioned. Like the main ingredients, these affect flavor profiles. Some people can be sensitive to aromatics or spicy ingredients. In other words, aromatics and other strong flavors could be a bad surprise. While reading through these examples, try to think of other aromatics or spices that you would mention.

| Mashed Potatoes | Garlic Mashed Potatoes |
|:---:|:---:|
| Roasted Corn | Roasted Corn<br>Browned Butter and Sage |
| Rice | Saffron Rice |
| Roasted Potatoes | Herb Roasted Potatoes<br>Rosemary and Shallot |
| Grilled Chimichurri Flank Steak<br>Marinated Prime Flank Steak marinated with Chimichurri | Grilled Chimichurri Flank Steak<br>Prime Flank Steak marinated with Coriander, Jalapeno and Onion Chimichurri |
| Baked Halibut with Roasted Tomato<br>Atlantic Halibut Fillet, Heirloom Tomatoes, Fresh Lemon and Thyme | Baked Halibut with Roasted Tomato and Fennel<br>Atlantic Halibut Fillet, Heirloom Tomatoes, Fragrant Fennel and Fennel Seed, Fresh Lemon and Thyme |

# Luxurious Dishes

Look over this list of foods. What ingredients should you mention? Use your imagination and describe the ingredients in a luxurious way.

| Food | Main Ingredients | Description |
|---|---|---|
| Yuk-Hei | Beef<br>Pear<br>Sesame Oil<br>Egg | |
| Galbi Jjim | | |
| Abalone Porridge | | |
| Spring Rolls | | |
| Dotorimuk | | |
| Spaghetti Carbonara | | |

## Other Menu Principles

After reviewing literature on menus (e.g. Dornenburg and Page 1996), a few things stand out. First, menus need balance between continuity and diversity. Continuity can mean serving the same cuisine or matching food styles. Diversity means different types of proteins and produce. Diversity also means non-repetition. That means that you should try not to repeat ingredients, flavors, tastes or cooking methods too much. Try to think about using contrasting tastes, flavors and textures between courses and when choosing accompaniments. Here are some example contrasts:

Light and Soft Textures / Rich and Full Textures

Subtle Flavors / Complex Flavors

Cold / Hot

Cooked / Raw

Creamy / Crispy

Crispy / Soft

Dry / Sauced

Heavy / Light

Mild to Spicy

Savory to Sweet

# Movement Through Courses

As you must be aware, different cuisines and meals are organized differently. Many American meals begin with salads and then serve heavier entrees. Some French meals begin with heavy entrees and end with salads. Many Chinese meals begin with cold dishes and end with hot. And, many Italian meals may feature starches before or between proteins. That said, many of the contrasts mentioned on the previous page can be found in each type of menu between and within courses. For practice, look over this menu and pick out each course's dominant tastes, flavors and textures. Think about how each course works together.

| Courses | Dominant Flavors, Tastes, Textures |
|---|---|
| **Roasted Pepper and Sundried Tomato Crostini** <br> Organic roasted red pepper, sundried tomato, fresh basil, homemade toasted crostini, light balsamic sauce | |
| **Mushroom Risotto** <br> Mixed wild mushroom, white wine, fresh butter and shallot risotto, finished with aged parmesan and chives | |
| **Veal Chop with Lemon Sage Sauce** <br> Broiled, free range veal loin chop with fresh sage and lemon | |
| **Egg Custard with Blackberries** <br> Freshly whipped traditional Italian custard with a hint of cognac and select organic blackberries | |

## A Traditional Korean Course

Here is an example four course Hanjeongsik meal. How would you describe the dishes on a menu? What are each dish's dominant flavors? Check out the Banchan on the next page and make suggestions for side dishes to recommend with each.

| Menu | Dominant Flavors, Tastes, Textures | With which side dishes? |
|---|---|---|
| **Red Bean Porridge** | | |
| **Grilled Beef Marinated with Ginseng** | | |
| **Rice Porridge with Abalone** | | |
| **Tea with Rice Cakes** | | |

## 'Banchan'

Write short descriptions for this list of side dishes.  Then recommend side dish pairings for the course options on the previous page.

### <u>Banchan</u>
Various traditional Korean accompaniments

Japchae

Muk Muchim

Dongchimi

Kim-chi

Jeon

Gamja Jorim

Gejang

Gosari Muchim

Munamul

*In Context*  **Seaside Restaurants and Strange Menus**

Read through the dialogue and answer or discuss the questions.

| | |
|---|---|
| Al | Hey, Ben. Did you check out the new restaurant by the beach? |
| Ben | I did, but I wasn't impressed. |
| Al | Oh? What was it like? |
| Ben | Well, the menu was confusing. It was a fusion menu, but it had traditional names. The menu took a long time to read. We couldn't decide, so we ordered the chef's recommended seafood course. |
| Al | How was the food? |
| Ben | This restaurant tries to mix different traditional foods from different cuisines in the same course menu. So, we had fried calamari, which is crispy, Italian style squid. They served that with a lemon and caper cream sauce. Then, they had tacos pescados, which is a fried cod fish taco with cabbage and sour cream. For dessert, they served churros, which are a fried Spanish donut with cinnamon and sugar. The churros had sweet cream on the side. The food was well-made using good ingredients, and you could taste the quality. But, the combination was terrible. |
| Al | The dishes sound a little repetitive. |
| Ben | That was one of the problems. Everything was fried and everything was served with a cream sauce. It was creative to try to have a fried seafood menu concept using cuisines from around the world. Creativity is good. But, I think they were trying to be too creative. The other problem was that the flavor |

profiles of the different cuisine styles clashed. There was no continuity.

Al      Are you going to go back? Maybe you should try ordering a la carte.

Ben     I might. They had great individual dishes. But, the chef definitely slept through his menu composition class.

## Strange Menus

As discussed throughout this section, course and set menus need balance and contrast, just like single dishes do. Think about how balance and contrast help to make great dining experiences as you answer or discuss the following questions.

• What were the problems with Ben's restaurant experience?

• Have you ever had a meal where the chef seemed like they were trying to be *too creative*? What was wrong with the food?

• How have you failed when trying to create a new dish or combination of dishes? What did you prepare? What did you learn from that?

## Apply It

Write a five course menu that uses various cooking methods and ingredients.
Try to include four of these contrasts between courses:

Light and Soft Textures / Rich and Full Textures

Subtle Flavors / Complex Flavors

| | |
|---|---|
| Cold / Hot | Dry / Sauced |
| Cooked / Raw | Heavy / Light |
| Creamy / Crispy | Mild / Spicy |
| Crispy / Soft | Savory / Sweet |

| Menu | Contrasts |
|---|---|
| | |

## Food for Thought

Food is a big part of the tourism industry. In fact, over 1/3 of travelers' and tourists' spending is dedicated to food (Herrerra, et al. 2012). Food can be more than just something that people enjoy when they travel, too. Food can be the reason why people travel to new places.

Experiences with a country's cuisine can seriously impact how people view a country (see: Gaztelumendi 2012). As a result, many governments spend a lot of money and do a lot of work promoting their cuisines around the world (see: Scarpato and Daniele 2003). Sometimes when promoting food, chefs change their food to be more palatable (or more delicious) to people in foreign markets. The same happens in restaurants that are marketed toward tourists: some tourist restaurants change their food for foreign travelers. However, most tourism experts suggest that to be successful, chefs should focus on providing authentic sensations and experiences, because that is what food tourists want (Gaztelumendi 2012, Herrera, et al. 2012).

Balancing authenticity and marketability can create difficult problems for chefs, particularly those working in tourist sectors like hotel restaurants. On the one hand, different people and their different tastes are a concern—if they don't like the food, it may change their opinions about visiting a country. On the other hand, many people are adventurous. They want to try authentically created foods in authentic settings.

## Questions for Thought

- Have you ever travelled abroad or do you want to travel abroad? What makes you want to travel?

- Would food cause you to want to (or not want to) visit a country?

- Do you think it is more important to create authentic dishes for people to try, or to create foods that are 'safer' for international visitors' tastes?

## Vocabulary from the Exercises

Although most sections ask you to decide on the vocabulary most important to you, here is some vocabulary that you can study to reinforce what you've learned. Then, you can check your understanding of the vocabulary on the next page.

| | | |
|---|---|---|
| A la carte | Entrées | Protein |
| Accomplished | Excite | Quality |
| Adventurous | Farm fresh | Raw |
| Aged | Fish Courses | Recommend |
| Alcoholic Beverages | Fixed | Repetition / Repetitive |
| Aperitifs | Flavor profile | Robust |
| Appetizer | Formal / Informal | Rotating |
| Authentic | Free-range | Salad |
| Beverages | Fresh | Season / Seasonal |
| Buffet offering | Fusion | Select |
| Casual | Global | Sensations |
| Cold Dishes | Heavy | Service style |
| Complex | Hors d'oeurves | Sides |
| Composition | Hot Dishes | Soup |
| Concern | International | Source |
| Confusing | Light | Standing options |
| Consistent | Luxurious | Starch |
| Continuity | Main courses | Starters |
| Course | Market availability | Subtle |
| Creative | Marketing / Marketability | Sweets |
| Cuisine | Motivation | Theme |
| Daily menu | Organic | Tourism |
| Desserts | Palate | Tourism sector |
| Diversity | Poultry | Wild |
| Dominant | Promote | |

## ✓ Check your Understanding

*dictatorial* /dɪktəˈtɔːrɪəl/ *adj.* like a dictator. **2** overbearing. **orially** *adv.* [Latin: related TATOR]
**diction** /ˈdɪkʃ(ə)n/ *n.* manner ciation in speaking or singing *dictio* from *dico dict-* say]
**dictionary** /ˈdɪkʃənərɪ/ *n.* (p book listing (usu. alphabetic explaining the words of a lar giving corresponding words i language. **2** reference book

Quiz yourself on the vocabulary by reading over the sentences below and choosing the words that fit the sentences best.

1. The menu needs (contrast / repetition). You should not braise every dish.

2. To create contrast, we should have a (hot dish / raw dish) after the hot pasta.

3. We should serve a simple flavor following this (complex / free-range) dish.

4. We want to promote our cuisine to tourists. We have to think about (creativity / marketability).

5. To complement this course's subtle flavors, have a more (light / robust) flavor in the next course. We should use an aged cheese.

6. My boss told me to pick a restaurant to impress the new clients. I think we should go somewhere (casual / formal).

7. I want some dessert. We should check out what (aperitifs / sweets) they offer.

8. We need some fixed entrees on the menu. We only have (daily menus / standing options).

9. The buffet offerings are (fixed / seasonal). Don't miss your chance.

10. We want to be marketable internationally. We should (creative / promote) our food on a global scale.

11. The restaurant was totally luxurious. It would be great for (formal / informal) meetings.

12. The (starters / entrees) were a bit too heavy. I don't know if I can eat the main course.

13. You can taste the quality of free range (red meat / salad).

14. The chef is both accomplished and adventurous. Her great skills can be seen in her menu. It is so (creative / confusing).

15. Are you sure the new menu matches our casual service style theme and concept? It seems like hors d'oeurves, and fish courses will be (confusing / continuity) for our customers.

16. To excite the palate, I recommend adding a few (luxurious / subtle) descriptions to the menu.

17. We need to promote our restaurant to healthy eaters. There is too much (red meat / white meat) on the menu.

18. Soups, sides, sweets—we have a menu to match everyone's (flavor profile / palate).

19. We have too much diversity. Tourists are confused by the menu. I think we should stick to one (cuisine / fusion).

20. After finishing this exercise, you probably need (an alcoholic beverage).

##  Unit 8  Menu Planning Wrap-Up Exercises and Projects

We've seen throughout these units how important details can be when explaining foods to people or when writing menus. Hopefully you've thought about how focusing on special ingredients can not only improve your dishes, but improve marketability. For example, when writing menus, most people know foods like 'steak'—you may feel that such a dish needs no detail. But, even for a dish like steak, details about the cut or quality of the beef can help to paint a picture of the food. Perhaps more important, by now you should also have explored how to detail new foods and traditional favorites from cultural cuisines to introduce them to guests and discuss them with colleagues.

This section provides exercises that reinforce and combine the concepts that you've worked with throughout the last few units. After thinking about the discussion questions, use the exercises to strengthen your understanding of the second section's concepts or use them to build further projects.

## Discussion

 Think about your own work and try to put yourself in the shoes of restaurant guests as you discuss or answer the following questions:

· How do seasonal ingredients affect how and what you cook?

· How do seasonal ingredients affect the foods that you go out to eat?

· What does continuity do for an eating experience? What are repetitive eating experiences like?

# Conceptualizing Vocabulary

Read through the descriptive words and decide which of the following categories they most identify with.

| | |
|---|---|
| a. Source (Where it's from) | d. Taste, Flavor or Texture |
| b. Ingredient | e. Part of a Meal |
| c. Preparation or Cooking Method | f. Unique/Special or Quality |

| | | |
|---|---|---|
| Alcoholic Beverages | Fresh | Prime |
| Aperitif | Ginger | Proteins |
| Appetizer | Grated | Removes |
| Beverages | Green onion | Rich |
| Bitter | Grilled | Roasted |
| Boiled | Homemade | Salad |
| Chewy | Hors d'oeurves | Salmon |
| Choice | Hot Dishes | Sautéed |
| Coffee | Japanese | Seafood |
| Cold Dishes | Korean | Select |
| Desserts | Lobster | Side Dishes |
| East sea | Main Course | Soup |
| Entrée | Marinated | Spicy |
| Entremets | Meat Course | Starter |
| Fish Course | Mediterranean | Sweets |
| Flank steak | Mushroom | Tender |
| Fluffy | Oily | Tossed |
| French | Onion | Traditional |

## Identifying Foods

For more practice, read over these international food descriptions and identify the foods that are being described.

1. _____ is an Italian pasta dish with large flat noodles layered with tomato sauce, meats or vegetables like spinach and cheeses and baked to finish. It's rich and savory, while the tomato sauce makes its flavor a little bright. It's delicious with salad, garlic bread and wine.

2. _____ is a classic American dessert. It has pastry loaded with sliced apples seasoned with cinnamon, nutmeg and sweetened with brown sugar. It's baked in the oven. The dough is flaky and the apples are sweet and aromatic. It's perfect with ice cream or a cup of coffee.

3. _____ is an appetizer with shredded lettuce and sliced vegetables, tossed with sauces or dressings and often topped with croutons, cheeses or other ingredients. It makes for a crisp, cool and light meal. It's great with a side of warm bread.

4. _____ is a savory and rich beef dish that consists of flaky pastry and minced mushrooms wrapped around tenderloin fillet. It's baked in the oven until the beef is cooked through and the pastry is crispy and flaky. It's nice with roasted vegetables or a bit of gravy.

5. _____ is a classic American sandwich. It consists of grilled ground beef, and people add whatever combinations of toppings they like. Some people add cheddar cheese, BBQ sauce, bacon and crispy fried onion rings. Other people like avocado, lettuce, tomato, pickles, mayonnaise and mustard. Grilled onions are a classic topping, too. Whatever the toppings, it's a great savory and fast meal and it's nice with crispy fried potatoes.

6. _____ is a classic, savory French vegetable dish with a variety of vegetables like eggplant, onion, peppers, zucchini and tomato. It has some bright aromatics like garlic, thyme and basil. The vegetables can be slow roasted or lightly simmered until it's a nice stew. It's great as a side dish to grilled meats, salads, omelets or just with crispy bread.

7. _____ is a great roasted meat dish with many national and regional varieties. This dish is often served with soft pita or flat breads. People add different vegetables like pickled cucumber, lettuce, and chili peppers. Some people like to add red onion, tomato, olives and some cheese. Most of the time, it has a creamy sauce. Generally, it's a savory, delicious and fast meal.

8. _____ is a savory Vietnamese noodle soup. It consists of beef or chicken bones simmered over a long time with many different aromatics like star anise, ginger, onion, coriander, fennel and clove. Before serving, you can pick your choice of chicken or beef: brisket, meat balls, rare flank steak, or tripe. It's great with pickled onions, bean sprouts, fresh basil, cilantro and a little bit of lime juice. It's often served with hoisin and chili sauce.

## Balancing a Single Plate Meal

Form a balanced main dish and some accompaniments or complements: a sauce, a side dish, and so on. Then explain why these items work together on the next page.

| What's on the plate? | What's in the glass? |
| --- | --- |
| | |

**Explanation:**

## Planning a Course Menu

Design a course menu for a cuisine that interests you, or create some fusion cuisine creations. Think about each dish's aromatics and how they work together, especially if planning a fusion course menu. Use some of the contrasts that were mentioned in units 6 and 7.

| Dish | Menu Presentation |
|---|---|
| **Describe the Dish** | |

| Dish | Menu Presentation |
|---|---|
| **Describe the Dish** | |

| Dish | Menu Presentation |
|---|---|
| **Describe the Dish** | |

## Planning a Special Buffet Section

Pick a special seasonal ingredient and plan a buffet section around it. You do not need to use the ingredient in every dish. But, you should include dishes that complement the special ingredient. Think about these questions as you do fill in the chart for this exercise on the next page:

• What is the buffet concept?

• What section are you planning your menu for?

• What is the special ingredient?

• What dishes would you choose to feature the ingredient's special properties?

• How do the other dishes in the section enhance the special ingredient?

| Buffet Concept: | Feature Ingredient: |
|---|---|
| Buffet Section: | |

| Feature Dishes (Special Ingredient) | Complementary Dishes/Items |
|---|---|
| | |

**Self—Study
Resources**

# Self-Study Resources

This section provides some space and extra exercises for you to check your knowledge on various ingredients, food items with culinary applications and whole foods and meals. After completing this section, you can use it as a mini reference guide. The following sections are included for quizzing yourself:

- Vegetables

- Fruit

- Herbs, Spices and Aromatics

- Fish

- Seafood

- Sauces

- Hotel Breakfasts

- Buffet Sections

## Vegetables

This list of vegetables is adapted from Ra's (2016) list of vegetables with culinary applications. Think about what each is, and whether it is a leafy vegetable, a stalk, a fruiting vegetable, a root, a flowering vegetable or a mushroom. Then, think of an example food or cuisine that uses the vegetable.

| Vegetable | Type of Vegetable | Example Dish / Cuisine |
|---|---|---|
| Artichoke | | |
| Arugula | | |
| Asparagus | | |
| Bamboo Shoot | | |
| Bok Choy | | |
| Broccoli | | |
| Brussel Sprout | | |
| Cabbage | | |
| Carrot | | |
| Cauliflower | | |

| Vegetable | Type of Vegetable | Example Dish / Cuisine |
|---|---|---|
| Celery | | |
| Chicory | | |
| Chinese cabbage | | |
| Corn | | |
| Cucumber | | |
| Eggplant | | |
| Enoki | | |
| Green Bean | | |
| Kale | | |
| Leek | | |
| Lettuce | | |
| Okra | | |
| Onion | | |
| Oyster Mushroom | | |
| Parsnip | | |

| Vegetable | Type of Vegetable | Example Dish / Cuisine |
|---|---|---|
| Potato | | |
| Pumpkin | | |
| Radicchio | | |
| Radish | | |
| Red Cabbage | | |
| Romaine Lettuce | | |
| Spinach | | |
| Squash | | |
| Sweet Potato | | |
| Taro | | |
| Tomato | | |
| Truffle | | |
| Turnip | | |
| Zucchini | | |

**Fruit**

This list of fruit is adapted from Ra's (2016) list of fruits with culinary applications. Think about what each is, and whether it most identifies as berry or berry-like, citrus, a melon, a pitted-fruit or a tropical fruit. Then, think about how you might serve the fruit or if you were to add it to a food, the sort of flavor it has.

| Fruit | Type of Fruit | Taste / How to Serve |
|---|---|---|
| **Apricot** | | |
| **Avocado** | | |
| **Banana** | | |
| **Blueberry** | | |
| **Cherry** | | |
| **Coconut** | | |
| **Cranberry** | | |
| **Date** | | |
| **Durian** | | |
| **Fig** | | |

| Fruit | Type of Fruit | Taste / How to Serve |
|---|---|---|
| Grapefruit | | |
| Honeydew | | |
| Jujube | | |
| Kiwi | | |
| Lemon | | |
| Mango | | |
| Mangosteen | | |
| Muskmelon | | |
| Orange | | |
| Papaya | | |
| Persimmon | | |
| Pineapple | | |
| Pomegranate | | |
| Raspberry | | |
| Strawberry | | |
| Tangerine | | |

## Herbs, Spices and Aromatics

This list of aromatics is adapted from Ra (2016). Think about what each is, a type of cuisine that the ingredient is commonly used in and a dish that uses the ingredient.

| Aromatic Herb / Spice / Vegetable | Types of Cuisines | Example Dishes |
|---|---|---|
| Allspice | | |
| Basil | | |
| Bay Leaf | | |
| Black Pepper | | |
| Cardamom | | |
| Caper | | |
| Cayenne Pepper | | |
| Celery | | |
| Chili Pepper | | |
| Chive | | |

| Aromatic Herb / Spice / Vegetable | Types of Cuisines | Example Dishes |
|---|---|---|
| Cinnamon | | |
| Cloves | | |
| Coriander | | |
| Cumin | | |
| Curry | | |
| Dill | | |
| Fennel | | |
| Garlic | | |
| Ginger | | |
| Horseradish | | |
| Marjoram | | |
| Mint | | |
| Mustard Seed | | |
| Nutmeg | | |
| Onion | | |

| Aromatic Herb / Spice / Vegetable | Types of Cuisines | Example Dishes |
|---|---|---|
| Oregano | | |
| Paprika | | |
| Parsley | | |
| Rosemary | | |
| Saffron | | |
| Sage | | |
| Shallot | | |
| Star Anise | | |
| Tarragon | | |
| Thyme | | |
| Turmeric | | |
| Vanilla | | |
| Wasabi | | |
| White Pepper | | |

**Fish**

This list of fish is adapted from Ra's (2016) list of fish with culinary applications. Think about what each fish is and a type of cuisine that usually uses the fish. Then, think of an example dish that uses the ingredient.

| Fish / Seafood Ingredient | Types of Cuisines | Example Dishes |
|---|---|---|
| Anchovy | | |
| Carp | | |
| Catfish | | |
| Cod | | |
| Eel | | |
| Flounder | | |
| Halibut | | |
| Herring | | |
| Mackerel | | |
| Minnow | | |

| Fish / Seafood Ingredient | Types of Cuisines | Example Dishes |
|---|---|---|
| Monk Fish | | |
| Mudfish | | |
| Puffer | | |
| Salmon | | |
| Sardine | | |
| Skate | | |
| Snapper | | |
| Sturgeon | | |
| Trout | | |
| Tuna | | |

# Seafood

This list of seafood is adapted from Ra's (2016) list of crustaceans, mollusks, cephalopods, Echinodermata and other types of delicious sea creatures with culinary applications. Think about what each ingredient is and a type of cuisine that usually uses the ingredient. Then, think of an example dish that uses the ingredient.

| Fish / Seafood Ingredient | Types of Cuisines | Example Dishes |
|---|---|---|
| Abalone | | |
| Clam | | |
| Cockle | | |
| Conch | | |
| Crab | | |
| Cray Fish | | |
| Cuttlefish | | |
| Langoustine | | |
| Lobster | | |

| Fish / Seafood Ingredient | Types of Cuisines | Example Dishes |
|---|---|---|
| Mussel | | |
| Octopus | | |
| Oyster | | |
| Scallop | | |
| Sea Cucumber | | |
| Sea Squirt | | |
| Short Necked Clam | | |
| Shrimp | | |
| Snail | | |

## Sauces

Think about the type of base that each of these sauces uses. Then, think about the types of cuisines that use the sauce, its dominant flavors and recommend it as an accompaniment for another dish.

| Sauce | Base | Types of Cuisines | Example Uses |
|---|---|---|---|
| Aioli | | | |
| Alfredo | | | |
| Béarnaise | | | |
| Bolognese | | | |
| Bordelaise | | | |
| Chateaubriand | | | |
| Chutney | | | |
| Demi-glace | | | |
| Espagnole | | | |
| Gravy | | | |

| Sauce | Base | Types of Cuisines | Example Uses |
|---|---|---|---|
| Hollandaise | | | |
| Italian Dressing | | | |
| Lemon Butter | | | |
| Marinara | | | |
| Mornay | | | |
| Peppercorn | | | |
| Pesto | | | |
| Ponzu | | | |
| Poulette | | | |
| Remoulade | | | |
| Salsa | | | |
| Sriracha | | | |
| Ssamgjang | | | |

# Hotel Breakfasts

The components of a hotel breakfast may be important for you to know depending on your working context. Thus, think about what goes into each of these breakfasts.

| Breakfast | Dishes |
|---|---|
| American | |
| Continental | |
| Vienna | |
| English | |

## Hotel Buffets

The components of a hotel buffet may be important for you to know depending on your working context. How many sections does a large hotel's buffet have in your working context? Take notes on the different sections and the types of foods that each section might serve.

| Section | Dishes |
|---|---|
|  |  |
|  |  |
|  |  |
|  |  |
|  |  |
|  |  |

# References

Ahn, Y-Y., Ahnert, S.E., Bagrow, J.P., Barabasi, A-L. (2011) 'Flavor network and the principles of food pairing', *Scientific Reports* 1:196, DOI: 10.1038/srep00196

Albala, K. (2011) *Food Cultures of the World Encyclopedia*, Vol. 1., Santa Barbara: Greenwood.

Blanding, M. (2011) The Yelp Factor: Are Consumer Reports Good for Business?. *Harvard School of Business Newsletter*, October 24. Retrieved from: http://hbswk.hbs.edu/item/the-yelp-factor-are-consumer-reviews-good-for-business

Daley, B. (2006, May 10) 'The Korean Challenge'. Retrieved from: http://articles.chicagotribune.com/2006-05-10/entertainment/0605090233_1_american-wine-lovers-korean-food-vodkalike

Dahmer, S.D. and Kahl, K.W. (2009) *Restaurant Service Basics*, 2nd ed. Hoboken: John Wiley and Sons.

Dornenburg, A. and Page, K. (1996) *Culinary Artistry*, New York: John Wiley and Sons.

Ferriss, T. (2012) *The 4-Hour Chef.* New York: Houghton Mifflin Harcourt.

Food Network Kitchen (2001) 'Apple Pie'. Retrieved from: http://www.foodnetwork.com/recipes/food-network-kitchen/apple-pie-recipe.

Garvey, M., Dismore, H., Dismore, A.G. (2011) *Running a Restaurant for Dummies*, 2nd ed. Hoboken: John Wiley and Sons, Inc.

Gaztelumendi, I. (2012) 'Global trends in food tourism'. In: Jordan, P. (Ed.), *Global Report on Food Tourism*, Vol. 4, pp. 10-15. Madrid: The World Tourism Organization (UNWTO).

Gisslen, W. (2006) *Professional Cooking for Canadian Chefs* 6th ed., Hoboken: John Wiley and Sons, Inc.

Gillingham, S.K. (2008, August 5) 'How To Write A Recipe Like A Professional', *The Kitchn.* Retrieved from: http://www.thekitchn.com/how-to-write-a-recipe-58522

Herrera, C.F., Herranz, J.B., Arilla, J.M.P. (2012) 'Gastronomy's importance in the development of tourism'. In: In: Jordan, P. (Ed.), *Global Report on Food Tourism*, Vol. 4, pp. 5-9. Madrid: The World Tourism Organization (UNWTO).

Hoffman, M. (2013) 'Is 'Red Wine with Meat, White with Fish' True?'. Retrieved from:

http://drinks.seriouseats.com/2013/03/ask-a-sommelier-red-with-meat-white-with-fish-rule-wine-pairing-advice.html

Hyslop, L. (2013, August 23) Potted Histories: Beef Wellington. Retrieved from: http://www.telegraph.co.uk/foodanddrink/10252209/Potted-histories-Beef-Wellington.html

Institute of Traditional Korean food (2007) *The Beauty of Korean Food*, Seoul: Hollym Corp.

Jeon, Y-C. (2012) 'Gastronomic Tourism in Korea: Globalizing Hansik'. In: Jordan, P. (Ed.), *Global Report on Food Tourism*, Vol. 4, pp. 36-37. Madrid: The World Tourism Organization (UNWTO).

Kim, A. [The Squishy Monster] (2012, December 5) 'KOREAN FOOD Kimchi Soup 김치 찌개 Recipe'. Retrieved from: https://www.youtube.com/watch?v=jAON_mUbp4c

Kittencal (N.D.) 'Kittencal's Lemon Shrimp Scampi With Angel Hair Pasta'. Retrieved from: http://www.food.com/recipe/kittencals-lemon-shrimp-scampi-with-angel-hair-pasta-169795

Lersch, M. (N.D.) 'Flavor Pairing', Retrieved from: http://blog.khymos.org/molecular-gastronomy/flavor-pairing/

Lersch, M. (2010) Texture -A hydrocolloid recipe collection (v.2.3). Retrieved from: http://blog.khymos.org/recipe-collection

Luca, M. (2011) 'Reviews, Reputation, and Revenue: The Case of Yelp.com'. *Harvard Business School*, Working Paper: 12-016.

Maangchi [Maangchi] (2007, November 26) 'Kimchi stew (kimchi-jjigae) and a bean sprout side dish'. Retrieved from: https://www.youtube.com/watch?v=sbmZjvjavaU

Michelin Guide Seoul (2016) 'Inspection Processes'. Retrieved from: http://guide.michelin.co.kr/en/about/inspection-processes/

Myhrvold, N, Young, C., Bilet, M. (2011) *Modernist Cuisine: The Art and Science of Cooking, Vol. 2: Techniques and Equipment*. Belevue: The Cooking Lab, LLC.

Oh, S., USDA Foreign Agricultural Service (2015) *Wine Market Report*, Seoul: U.S. Agricultural Trade Office. Retrieved from: http://gain.fas.usda.gov/Recent%20GAIN%20Publications/Wine%20Market%20Report_Seoul%20ATO_Korea%20-%20Republic%20of_2015-07-20.pdf

Ra, Y-S. (2016) *Basic Western Cuisine*. Seoul: Baeksan Publishing Co.

Scarpato, R. and Daniele, R. (2003) 'New Global Cuisine: tourism, authenticity and sense of place in postmodern gastronomy'. In: Hall, M., Sharples, L., Mitchell, R., Macionis, N., Cambourne, B. (Eds.), *Food Tourism Around the World*, pp. 296-313. Oxford: Butterworth-Heinenmen.

Strange, J. [James Strange] (2013, July 5) 'Korean Cooking Kimchi jjigae (kimchi stew) Recipe / World of Flavor'. Retrieved from: https://www.youtube.com/watch?v= FwpR3aU68Z0

The Culinary Institute of America (2006) *The Professional Chef*, Hoboken: John Wiley & Sons, Inc.

Tice, C. (2013, November 24) 'Bootstrap Startup: Inside a $13k Restaurant Opening', R etrieved from: http://www.forbes.com/sites/caroltice/2013/11/24/boostrap-start ups-13k-restaurant-opening/#4e2af4931bf4

Yee, K. K., Sukumaran, S.K., Kotha, R., Gilbertson, T.A., Margolskee, R.F. (2011) 'Glucose transporters and ATP-gated K+ (KATP) metabolic sensors are present in type 1 taste receptor 3 (T1r3)-expressing taste cells, *PNAS* 108/13: 5431-5436.

Zimmerman, L. (2015, July 6) *Korean food can be paired with a wine*, but it's not easy. Retrieved from: http://www.sfexaminer.com/korean-food-can-be-paired-with-wine-but-its-not-easy/

# About the Authors

*Jonathan Huynh* (조나단 휜) is an assistant professor in Shin Ansan University's Hotel Culinary Arts department. He has a decade of professional experience teaching and designing course materials for specific academic and professional purposes. He received his Master of Arts degree in Applied Linguistics and TESOL from the University of Leicester (UK) and his Bachelor of Arts degree in English Literature from San Francisco State University (USA).

*Ra, Young Sun* (나영선) is a professor in Shin Ansan University's Hotel Culinary Arts department. He has served as President of the Culinary Professor Society of Korea, President of the Korea Chefs Association, President of the Korean Journal of Culinary, International Judge of the World Association Chefs Society (WACS) and Chef at the Grand Hyatt Hotel, Seoul, and Grand Intercontinental Hotel, Seoul.

# Culinary English Skill Builder 조리영어 스킬 빌더

2017년 3월 10일 초판 1쇄 발행
2020년 2월 10일 초판 2쇄 발행

**지은이** Jonathan Huynh · Ra Young-Sun
**펴낸이** 진욱상
**펴낸곳** 백산출판사
**교 정** 편집부
**본문디자인** 편집부
**표지디자인** 오정은

**등 록** 1974년 1월 9일 제1-72호
**주 소** 경기도 파주시 회동길 370(백산빌딩 3층)
**전 화** 02-914-1621(代)
**팩 스** 031-955-9911
**이메일** edit@ibaeksan.kr
**홈페이지** www.ibaeksan.kr

**ISBN** 979-11-5763-342-5  93740
**값 18,000원**